K. Davies

Finishing the Race

Reading 2 Timothy Today

Christopher Green

AQUILA
PRESS

A book by Aquila Press

Published June 2000

Aquila Press, PO Box A287, Sydney South NSW 1235, Australia

National Library of Australia
ISBN 1 875861 82 3

Printed in Australia by Southwood Press Pty. Limited

Foreword

Chris Green is one of the leaders of younger evangelical ministers in the United Kingdom and it is a pleasure to welcome this first commentary in our series from an author outside Australia.

Upon ordination in the Church of England Chris had extensive parish experience prior to his appointment as Vice Principal of Oak Hill College. Chris is a gifted preacher and teacher who regularly ministers to university groups and in the Cornhill Training Course. He plays an active role in diocesan life as well as in nationwide evangelical organizations.

Chris Green's breadth of scholarship and biblical learning tempered by extensive pastoral experience equip him well to write a commentary on Paul's Second Letter to Timothy. The apostle wrote to his younger colleague out of the crucible of suffering into which both were plunged, in particular into the pain of rejection by those who are now turning from the 'pattern of truth' and the moral standards of the Gospel of Christ. This commentary on Paul's words enters deeply into their meaning, both then and now. Its application to us is powerful and relevant.

I am confident that our author, moved by the Spirit of Christ, will bring alive to us the inspiring passion of Paul's original letter.

DR PAUL BARNETT
Series Editor

For the Cornhill Training Course

Contents

Preface

One of my greatest pleasures and privileges in recent years has been to be involved in teaching at the Cornhill Training Course in London. Under the guiding hands of David Jackman and Dick Lucas, hundreds of young men and women have been taught the principles of handling the Bible accurately, evangelism, youth work and church life. The course has grown from a handful to nearly one hundred students, and as the ex-students have begun to move into positions of church leadership around the world, it has been my annual responsibility to teach 2 Timothy to a roomful of Timothys. Together, as I have spoken and they have listened, discussed, questioned and suggested, we have come face to face with the issues of ministry, failure, and suffering for the gospel. They cannot imagine what they have contributed to what is in these covers, and it is a great honour for me to dedicate this book to them. As I said to them so many times, and as I imagine they now need to rediscover for themselves as they step up to the front line, 'Timothy was normal'.

Anyone who writes on issues to do with churches, leadership, division and disloyalty must expect the spotlight to fall on his own church, so I want to thank the members of Emmanuel Church, Tolworth for their love, understanding and support over a number of years, some of which have not been easy for us. I need to underline for the sake of their public reputation that this is not a book written out of the frustration of trying to lead them!

My wife, Sharon, has been a wonderful encouragement for me to finish, and our son, Edward, has been a delightful excuse to delay. Paul Barnett has been a source of support, patience and numerous helpful suggestions.

CHRISTOPHER GREEN

Reading 2 Timothy Today (1)

1

Why read 2 Timothy?

In 1415 the church reformer, Jan Hus, was arrested, tried, condemned and sentenced to burn at the stake for his heresy, a heresy which would be seen today as merely preaching the Bible clearly to a packed church in Prague. As the flames engulfed him he quoted Psalm 25:2:

In you, I trust, O God,
do not let me be ashamed,
do not let my enemies triumph over me.

Approximately one third of the Christian church today must operate in conditions of secrecy, under similar threats of punishment and extermination. That means that of Christianity's current 1,750 million adherents, over 500 million believe while experiencing persecution. Whether it is in conditions of outright hostility and violence, or the more subtle pressures of job insecurity or difficulty finding food and housing, many Christians find that their faith causes them and their families trouble.

Under those circumstances, what would persuade someone to become a Christian, or, when the pressure increases, to remain one? How many would turn up to your home group under such conditions? Even more sharply, what could possibly persuade a Christian like you to attract the attention of the local police by becoming a Christian leader? Or as close friends and church members begin to keep a discreet distance in order to preserve their own safety, what could persuade you to remain a leader? Where does someone under close observation, harassment, arrest, and the threat of execution, draw the strength to say with Hus, *Do not let me be ashamed?*

The answer lies in Paul's explanation of the spiritual dynamics of Christian ministry, outlined here in 2 Timothy. Being ashamed about the gospel is a key issue in the letter, as Paul, deserted, imprisoned and anxious for the future leadership of the churches he has planted, shares with Timothy the secret of his own determination. *Of this gospel,* he writes, *I was appointed a herald and an apostle and a teacher. That is why I am suffering as I am.* ***Yet I am not ashamed,*** *because I know whom I have believed, and am convinced that he is able to guard what I have entrusted to him for that day* (1:11–12). Paul speaks warmly of Onesiphorus, the one Christian from Ephesus who had made a courageous effort to locate his cell in Rome: *he often refreshed me* ***and was not ashamed*** *of my chains* (1:16). A large part of this letter is concerned with courage, backbone and an iron will.

Most people in our culture would not relate to that issue at all. If they are not Christians they see our message as irrelevant, archaic and incomprehensible. In an increasingly pluralistic, tolerant and secular age the gospel is embarrassingly exclusive and God-obsessed, built on truth-claims that deny others' right to claim truth. In that context, what could possibly persuade a young Christian to give up an attractive career and enter full-time Christian ministry? Why take up leadership as Christians are dwindling in importance, and only politically-minded campaign groups and publicity-seeking heretics seem to grab the headlines? Even those who lead large churches will say, if they are candid, that their task is much harder than it was twenty years ago, and churches with large front doors discover they have large back doors too; church members are fickle, and move from one congregation to another at the rumour of the latest blessing of God.

What persuades people to become – and remain – that increasingly odd item, a Christian? And, when full-time Christian ministry no longer grants respectability, or even a polite hearing, why should the best of the young become church leaders? And as they see their peers gain in influence and affluence, why should they remain in their ministries?

Again, 2 Timothy speaks to our age and our churches. People had deserted Paul not only because of political pressure but also because he and his message were an embarrassment. They and their ambient culture were *lovers of themselves, ... money* (and) *pleasure* (3:2,4), who did not care for *endurance, persecutions* (and) *sufferings* (3:10–11). They were drifting from his churches to newer, less demanding but more exciting, ministries. Well known Christians like Demas (4:10, see Colossians 4:14), Phygelus and Hermogenes (1:15) were deserting him, and now Paul is concerned that even Timothy might distance himself as well. Hence the call to Timothy, *Do not be **ashamed** to testify about our Lord, or **ashamed** of me his prisoner. But join with me in suffering for the gospel, by the power of God* (1:8).

Suffering for the authentic gospel is inevitable, but of course it proves nothing, and by contrast many said – and still say – that visible success is the great proof of God's blessing. Hymenaeus and Philetus are examples of that approach (2:17–18). By contrast, Paul places his major calls to loyalty in the context of God's Judgment Day (1:12–13; 4:1–2, 5–8, 14–18) where the evaluation for success in ministry is done outside this world.

Whether we are young Christians considering the cost of Christian ministry, older Christian leaders beginning to lose our cutting edge, concerned members who see, year by year, fewer people turning up to church, or despairing watchers of the wider Christian scene who see cleverly marketed errors luring gullible believers into parting with their cash, 2 Timothy has some remarkably relevant things to say. If you are a leader in some capacity you will discover what Christian ministry is, and is not. If you train younger Christians for future responsibilities, you will discover what to teach them so that they will last the course and train others properly in their turn. If you are a church member you should know that in the letter's closing verse, the words *Grace be with you* are plural: Paul expects Timothy's church to be reading this letter over his shoulder. Read this letter over your pastor's shoulder, see the pressures that your leaders are under, and consider how you can pray for them and keep them going.

Above all, 2 Timothy should encourage us. If we are honest we know the inconsistencies in our own hearts, and we have learned the hard way that we are not to be relied upon as the key to world revival. Every church leader has at some time or other wept like Timothy (1:4), whether over the gullibility of the church, the hardness of the surrounding culture, the responsibilities that crush us, the harshness of opposition or our own inability to live up to the high ideals we started out with. Every church leader who has wept and considered giving up in despair – and that is probably every honest church leader – can learn that it is possible to say with Paul, *I have fought the good fight, I have finished the race, I have kept the faith* (4:7).

STUDY, DISCUSSION AND PRAYER

1. Read through 2 Timothy noting examples and themes of loyalty or disloyalty. What are your initial impressions about the central concerns of the letter?

2. Who are the people most similar to Timothy in your church? How can you pray for them with greater understanding?

2

Why read *this* book?

After a period of relative neglect there has been a recent surge of interest in the Pastoral letters, and there are several excellent commentaries now available. The most thorough are by George W. Knight III and I. Howard Marshall who both consider every detail of the text. Briefer and still excellent commentaries have been written by (among others) John Stott, Gordon Fee, Thomas D. Lea and Hayne P. Griffin Jr., and Philip Towner. As so often, the letter was well explained by John Calvin, and in particular by his sermons on the letter. (Unfortunately they are only available in a facsimile of the 1579 edition, which makes them almost useless unless they are doggedly read aloud!) For the details of Paul's imprisonment, Brian Rapske has written a stimulating study for the multi-volume 'The Book of Acts in its First Century Setting' series.

So why is there a place for this book? Partly because it is brief, and that is important at a time when time seems short for everyone. This series is aimed at the busy preacher and home group leader who should find the explanation and the study questions accessible and thought provoking.

That means there will be many points of detail which will have to be glossed over, and where the longer commentaries above will show their value.

A second reason for this book is that longer commentaries can often lose sight of the principal themes because of the detail they are required to explain, even when the text is as brief as 2 Timothy. This exposition tries to keep one eye above the words and sections, and look out for what has been called the 'melodic line' or 'theme tune' of the letter.

So a question which will continually surface is, 'Why is this thought *here*?', meaning not only, 'Why is it in 2 Timothy as opposed to Titus or James?', but, 'Why does it come here, at this point in the letter, after what we have seen so far, and leading up to the next point?'. A number of famous verses have a much sharper focus when understood in their proper setting, and apparent digressions suddenly become central.

STUDY, DISCUSSION AND PRAYER

2 Timothy is a letter to be thought about, as Paul himself says: *Reflect on what I am saying, for the Lord will give you insight into all this* (2:7). So before reading through this book, take time to read through the letter several times. The version assumed here will be the New International Version.

In order to set the tone there are some introductory sections which may prove helpful, pointing out some of the principal concerns and thoughts. They do not have discussion or prayer pointers.

Just as a great symphony or painting only begins to reveal its secrets when we immerse ourselves in it, so the Bible repays careful, repeated, prayerful thought. And God promises to give the insight that our own unaided minds could not grasp.

3

The myth of 'Timid Timothy'

The character of the man that Paul was writing to sets the tone of this letter, and also determines how much we can learn from it. Timothy had been brought up in a Jewish home, and probably both his mother and grandmother became Christians (1:5). His father's belief is not mentioned, so it is unlikely he was a Christian. Although Timothy's conversion is not recorded he was clearly a keen Christian whose potential as an evangelist and pastor had commended him to both his own church leaders and to Paul (Acts 16:1–2). Paul's use of him in planting and strengthening churches speaks strongly of his personal and spiritual maturity.

However, in 1:7 Paul reminds Timothy that *God did not give us a spirit of* ***timidity****, but a spirit of power, of love and of self-discipline,* and it is almost irresistible to underline one word and refer to 'Timid Timothy'. The alliteration is very tempting. But it probably should be resisted on a number of grounds, however sympathetic we may feel towards him. Since this is a widely held view of the man, and since it colours the way the entire letter is read, it is worth airing the problem now. It also gives a chance for a view of the man Paul called his *dear son* (1:2).

THE CASE FOR 'TIMID TIMOTHY'

There are a number of elements that make up the case for Timothy being a slightly bashful young man pushed beyond the limits of his competence by Paul. They can be grouped into five concerns:

His youth

It is clear from 1 Timothy that when that letter was written Timothy would have been classed as younger rather than older. *Do not rebuke an older man harshly, but exhort him as if he were your father. Treat younger men as brothers, older women as mothers, and younger women as sisters, with absolute purity* (1 Timothy 5:1-2). At that stage he clearly falls into the younger generation, which causes him some difficulty when confronting condescending false teachers, for Paul instructs him, *Don't let anyone look down on you because you are young* (1 Timothy 4:12). Perhaps not much time had elapsed between the two letters, because in 2 Timothy he is told to *Flee the evil desires of youth* (2:22). Maybe as a young leader faced with mounting opposition and dwindling attendance he began to doubt his readiness for leadership. And maybe his church began to doubt it too.

His frailty

Again from 1 Timothy, he appears not to have been robust enough for the task in hand. *Stop drinking only water, and use a little wine because of your stomach and your frequent illnesses* (1 Timothy 5:23). Perhaps his natural diffidence was being encouraged by not being able to put in the hours required to lead a church. Perhaps he began to worry that the spread of false teaching in the church was the result of his ineffective leadership.

His fearfulness

When Paul wrote to the Corinthians he made explicit his instructions about Timothy: *If Timothy comes, see to it that he has nothing to fear while he is with you* (1 Corinthians 16:10). Perhaps he was not cut out for the more robust and demanding elements of Christian work.

His tears

Recalling your tears, I long to see you (1:4) wrote Paul. The young man, unwell and lonely, out of his depth and feeling that Paul blamed him for his failure to deal with the error of Hymenaeus (1 Timothy 1:20, 2 Timothy 2:17) had begun to crack under the pressure.

His timidity

This seems the natural conclusion to what has gone before. There have been other elements added to this brew (an absent and unbelieving father with Paul as a substitute, for example) but even as it stands it is powerful and devastating. So Paul was frustrated and anxious, but impotent in his prison. All he could do was tell Timothy to confront the problem head on. *God did not give us a spirit of timidity* (1:7).

The nature of the relationship between the two men is clearly crucial, and the writings of the commentators reflect that. Occasionally, a commentator writing from an academic background will see the relationship as one between a teacher and a pupil, with Paul as an elderly don fussing over the misbehaviour of a beloved, but sickly, favourite student. Others write (much more plausibly) from within a context of church leadership, but for some it becomes clear that they identify with Timothy so much that their past hurts, failures and frustrations are read into his. We need to tread carefully here, for there is obviously something about his plight which chimes naturally with those of us who know the price of leadership, and yet the letter is to and about Timothy rather than us.

It is possible to give a different account of the five points above and, by taking other elements into account as well, come to a different conclusion about this engaging young man. The conclusion, however, will make this letter more, not less, relevant.

THE CASE AGAINST 'TIMID TIMOTHY'

His youth?

The verses from 1 Timothy are telling but of course they relate to that letter rather than this, and it is difficult to date with any precision the timing between the two, which could well have been several years. The reference in 2 Timothy to *flee the evil desires of youth* (2:22) will become clearer in context, but here it is important to notice that the desires are inappropriate. Timothy is either being told to grow up or, more probably, to act his age. In addition, the word *youth* commonly meant up to forty. The early Christian writer Irenaeus wrote that *Thirty is the first stage of a young man's age, and extends to forty, as all will admit* (Avd. Haer. 2.22.5).

It is not necessary to see Timothy as a teenager out of his depth. The word, as it is used in 2 Timothy, is capable of meaning someone significantly older. A friend of mine said how pleased he was to have had his fortieth birthday because it meant that people at his church would take him seriously! Perhaps the issue here is that because of his comparative youth Timothy lacks authority.

But whatever his youth, Timothy was undoubtedly experienced. He had worked and suffered alongside Paul on many journeys, and that could well mean he was older than we might think, and quite possibly older than his years.

His frailty?

The church in Ephesus seems to have had problems with both indulgence (1 Timothy 3:3) and asceticism (1 Timothy 4:3), and steering Timothy and his church through that minefield would make Paul concerned for him. It is quite possible, after all, that Timothy's *frequent illnesses* (1 Timothy 5:23) were caused by too rigorous a diet, and Paul calls him to relax and ease up for the sake of his health. Nonetheless, to repeat the obvious, this reference is to 1 rather than 2 Timothy, and Paul is unlikely to have made a weakling his travelling companion during his arduous years of travel and church planting.

His fearfulness?

The hostility to Paul of some in Corinth is clear from the two existing letters. Some would have no doubt been more aggressive towards Paul's representative than to Paul himself. If Paul had to face charges of being *'timid' when face to face with you, but 'bold' when away* (2 Corinthians 10:1) it is not surprising that he is anxious for Timothy, and that Timothy is apprehensive about going. To be Paul's delegate and receive the direct response to 1 Corinthians in person, and be answerable for it, would make even the most thick-skinned think twice. So Paul wraps his apostolic protection around Timothy, not because Timothy is unnaturally timid, but because the Corinthians are unnaturally aggressive. *If Timothy comes, see to it that he has nothing to fear while he is with you, for he is carrying on the work of the Lord, just as I am. No one, then, should refuse to accept him. Send him on his way in peace so that he may return to me. I am expecting him along with the brothers* (1 Corinthians 16:10–11).

His tears?

Perhaps Timothy was too soft and not cut out for ministry, but in that case every other Christian leader who has wept for the church faces the same charge. Watching the stubborn refusal of false teachers to repent, even after discipline, and then seeing a congregation leave to follow that same error would be an extremely frustrating experience. Those whose ministries have seen only growth, conversion and maturity may find Timothy too weak. Those who have seen churches *turn their ears away from the truth and turn aside to myths* (4:4), and agonised over immature Christians who are *always learning but never able to acknowledge the truth* (3:7) while *evil men and impostors ... go from bad to worse* (3:13) will find him all too real.

TIMOTHY

Timothy was an exceptionally close colleague of Paul. He is mentioned as one of Paul's co-writers for seven of his letters (Romans 16:21, 2 Corinthians 1:1, Philippians 1:1, Colossians 1:1, 1 Thessalonians 1:1, 2 Thessalonians 1:1, Philemon 1:1). Apart from occasional errands and enforced separations (1 Corinthians 4:17, Acts 17:14) Timothy seems to have been a permanent member of Paul's close team.

He came from Lystra (modern Zostera, in southern Turkey), a Roman colony and a centre of education and culture. His father was Greek while his mother, Eunice and grandmother, Lois, were Jewish, and he obviously had an imprint of both cultures from an early age. His mother and grandmother had taught him the Jewish scriptures (3:15), but his father had not allowed him to be circumcised (Acts 16:3). At some stage Eunice had become a Christian (Acts 16:1).

Timothy was also converted, possibly on one of Paul's visits to Lystra in the late 40s AD (either Acts 14:6 or 14:21) which may be why Paul can call him *my true son in the faith* (1 Timothy 1:2). He made rapid and impressive progress as a Christian, and on a return visit to Lystra Paul heard that the Christians at both his home church and nearby Iconium (modern Konya) *spoke well of him* (Acts 16:2). The two men clicked, and Timothy joined Paul and Silas' team. They travelled to Troas, where they were joined by Luke, and then into mainland Europe.

While Paul was in Athens Timothy was sent on his first extended solo mission to encourage and strengthen the young church in Thessalonica (1 Thessalonians 3:2). He rejoined Paul in Corinth (Acts 18:5) and seems to have spent most of the next eighteen months there with Paul, and most of the subsequent three years with him in Athens. During this time Timothy was sent on an extended trip to Macedonia (Acts 19:22), and perhaps this was the time he was sent into the difficult waters of the church in Corinth

(1 Corinthians 4:17). Paul's comments in that letter must be read in the light of the known hostility of some of the Corinthians to Paul. It was the nature of that church, not the nature of Timothy or Paul, which made grown men tremble.

Timothy was with Paul on his last journey to Jerusalem (Acts 20:4), and was obviously with him as he wrote subsequently from prison to the churches in Philippi (Philippians 1:1), Colossae (Colossians 1:1) and to Philemon (Philemon 1). At that stage Paul was anticipating an early release, and Timothy was his emissary. He wrote to the Philippians, *I hope in the Lord Jesus to send Timothy to you soon, that I also may be cheered when I receive news about you. I have no one else like him, who takes a genuine interest in your welfare. For everyone looks out for his own interests, not those of Jesus Christ. But you know that Timothy has proved himself, because as a son with his father he has served with me in the work of the gospel. I hope, therefore, to send him as soon as I see how things go with me.* (Philippians 2:19–23). That was presumably in the context of the trials and journeys that brought Paul to Rome at the end of Acts.

Only two more events from Timothy's life are known with any certainty. He was placed in charge of the church in Ephesus (1 Timothy 1:3) which turned out to be a hard task, as 2 Timothy shows. And at some stage Timothy was himself in a prison cell, because there is news about him from the anonymous author of Hebrews: *I want you to know that our brother Timothy has been released. If he arrives soon, I will come with him to see you* (Hebrews 13:23).

Perhaps, then, new words are needed to describe Timothy. The way his church leaders and Paul identified him might make him **talented Timothy**; his years of travelling with Paul made him **trained Timothy**; **trusted Timothy** was sent to defuse that spiritual bomb in Corinth. But in 2 Timothy the problem emerges that even a man as gifted as this might find the pressure too great and be tempted to give up his ministry as Paul had described it to him. The cumulative cost was proving too great for

tempted Timothy. Sentimentalism makes a bad ally in reading this letter, and those who do not fall into the trap of 'timid Timothy' quite often fall into the opposite but equally sentimental one of 'talented Timothy' who simply could not fail, and for whom all the warnings are hypothetical. But Timothy, for all his gifts, training and experience was undoubtedly facing a major crisis as Paul wrote this letter.

It is that crisis which makes the letter so sharp for Christian leaders today. Either of the sentimental readings will make Timothy an unusual man, whether unusually weak or unusually strong. But an unsentimental reading shows a different man, a normal man, a Christian leader like every other. **Typical Timothy**. The pressure he faced, the rebukes and assurances he received from Paul together with the theological purpose he is re-equipped with, are all points to which any minister can relate.

Timid Timothy?

The word *timid* will be dealt with in its place (1:7), but the conclusion of the majority of commentators is that *cowardice* (as the NRSV puts it) would be a much better translation. Unfortunately *timid* has become almost permanently associated with Timothy because of the handiness of the phrase 'Timid Timothy', and because it makes Timothy sound gentle, likeable and a bit like we imagine ourselves to be. *Cowardice* is a much less diplomatic word. But it is the right word, because Paul is not criticising Timothy's personality, but identifying the danger that Timothy will, at a critical moment, drop out of the responsibilities of Christian leadership because the personal cost will be too high. That makes 2 Timothy relevant to more than the few shrinking violets. No matter how long they have been Christians (and Timothy has been a Christian *from infancy* [3:15]) or how well trained (and Timothy had been trained by a notoriously perfectionist Paul [Acts 15:36–40]) people can suddenly meet such a spasm of cowardice. Everyone needs the warning and the encouragement.

4

The myth of 'Pessimistic Paul'

At the time he wrote 2 Timothy Paul was in prison. That is, he was not under the house arrest at the end of Acts, but in chains and lost somewhere in the legal corridors of Rome. Onesiphorus had *searched hard for me until he found me* (1:17) – which makes the traditional site of the Mamartine prison in Rome unlikely, because it is far too prominent on the Capitol Hill. It would have stood out like the Tower of London or Sydney Harbour Bridge, and even in ancient Rome it was a tourist site. Paul was somewhere else in that sprawling city, entirely dependent on an increasingly small group of associates for food and clothing.

But what did he expect to happen? The usual assumption is that he knew he was about to die and that 2 Timothy is his last message from death row. *For I am already being poured out like a drink offering, and the time has come for my departure. I have fought the good fight, I have finished the race, I have kept the faith. Now there is in store for me the crown of righteousness, which the Lord, the righteous Judge, will award to me on that day* (4:6–8).

Couple the imminence of unpleasant death with Paul's knowledge of the growth of false teaching and doubts over the reliability of even his most trusted lieutenant, and 2 Timothy reads like a gloomy analysis of the future. It could be that things were better out in the wider world than Paul could imagine from his unpleasant vantage point, and 2 Timothy is the thinking of a disappointed man who saw his life in retrospect as a failure.

There are clues, though, that this might not be the correct view and that, even granted the theological error and the desertions, both past and possible, Paul was optimistic about the future.

OPTIMISTIC ABOUT THE GOSPEL

Given the downbeat way many read 2 Timothy, it needs to be underlined that Paul was extremely positive about God's work in the world. After all, these are the *last days* (3:1), which means every day is the gospel day, the day of salvation, even if that time is periodically marked by *terrible times.* These are the days when Jesus Christ *has destroyed death and brought life and immortality to light through the gospel* (1:10), and God's purpose is that *all the Gentiles might hear it* (4:17), even if the price of that is Paul's own life. Paul could look back to the *appearing of our Saviour, Christ Jesus* (1:10) and encourage Timothy to be one of those who minister *in view of his* future *appearing and his kingdom* (4:1). So even though the letter has dark themes, its undergirding theology is clearly upbeat and expansionist.

OPTIMISTIC ABOUT THE CHURCH

Despite the creeping rot of error and the frustrating gullibility of the churches to fall for it, Paul is convinced that God knows what is happening and will not let the difficulties continue to the point where there are no more Christians. *God's solid foundation stands firm, sealed with this inscription: 'The Lord knows who are his,' and, 'Everyone who confesses the name of the Lord must turn away from wickedness'* (2:19). Even though Paul may have doubts about particular congregations and their leaders, he has no doubt about God's care and protection of his people as a whole. The false teachers *will not get very far* (3:9).

OPTIMISTIC ABOUT HIMSELF

At the end of the letter Paul discusses some of his plans (it will be argued below that these are central to the letter and not mere 'closing remarks'). Even that fact should surprise us. What is a man on death row doing making plans? Not only that, the plans are for the rest of the year (4:21). So even if he is expecting to die, he is not expecting to die immediately.

Then there is the curious element that having strengthened Timothy for ministry where he is, he closes the letter by wanting Timothy by his side in Rome (4:21). If we rule out that he was absentminded, or simply soft, we need to explain why a hard-headed church planter would pull Timothy away from active and desperately needed ministry in Ephesus into a lengthy and expensive journey to join Paul and Luke in Rome. Not only that, he is to *bring Mark* with him (4:11) and collect Paul's travelling *cloak* (4:12). Sentimentalism, once again, pictures an elderly man, lonely, cold and on the edge of death, wanting to be reunited with his old friends one last time. A different look at the scene, though, might suggest that Paul plus Timothy plus Luke plus Mark would be a formidable team for planning evangelism and church planting. Mark is wanted by Paul *because he is helpful to me in … ministry* (4:11, the word *my* is not in the Greek). Perhaps Paul wanted his travelling coat because he hoped he might travel.

Reading 4:17–18 in this light gives it a much more positive feel: *But the Lord* ***stood*** *at my side and* ***gave*** *me strength, so that through me the message might be fully proclaimed and all the Gentiles might hear it. And I* ***was*** *delivered from the lion's mouth. The Lord* ***will*** *rescue me from every evil attack and will bring me safely to his heavenly kingdom. To him be glory for ever and ever. Amen.* Reflecting on previous elements of his trial and seeing how God delivered him then, it is possible to take the next phrase in one of two ways: either he says that Rome's attacks may kill him but that will not thwart God's plans, or that he expects to be rescued from the attack, and also be safely in God's kingdom. The possible Old Testament background to these verses is given in the comments below.

None of this removes Paul's expectation of death. He sees himself as approaching the end of his ministry, having passed the test of acknowledging Christ before Caesar's courts. It is up to the next generation to continue ministry after the pattern he has laid down. Nor does this reading alter the main thrust of the letter.

This optimistic view may not be correct. However, if it makes someone who has read the letter for years as a tearful and frail farewell reread it through different lenses, then even if that reader is not finally convinced, new light may have been shed.

5

Two cities

2 Timothy is not just a letter between two men in widely different circumstances, but between two cities. Both have implications for how the letter is to be read.

ROME

Rome was the proud and successful capital of its vast empire, and was its administrative hub, run by an estimated 20,000 slave officials. The wealthy governing families lived in extensive palaces on the famous seven hills, and the remaining million or so lived mostly in crowded and dangerous tenement blocks. To be born a citizen of Rome, as Paul was (Acts 22:28) gave enormous prestige across the entire Mediterranean world and beyond, and gave him an unrivalled freedom to travel. Geographically, financially, legally, politically and militarily, Rome was the centre to which all roads ran.

It is little wonder that Paul planned to go to such a city. In Ephesus he seems to have adopted the pattern of working in a central place, and allowing the movement of traffic to carry potential converts into his path, and the gospel to go out with them (Acts 19:9–10). Rome, even more than Ephesus, was the natural arena for such a ministry, and it had long been in his mind to visit the church there (Romans 1:13; 15:23). From Galatians 2:7–9 it seems to have been Paul's desire to work steadily westwards, finally reaching Rome (Romans 1:13). His ambition had a deeper motivation than merely visiting a church or reaching some non-Christians. Although he had a desire to *visit Rome* it was an essential element of his commission as an apostle that he should go there. Jesus told him *'Take courage! As you have testified about me in Jerusalem, so you must also testify in Rome'* (Acts 23:11). In some way, Paul's apostleship to the Gentiles was crystallised in a particular responsibility to bear witness to Christ in the heart of Caesar's power base. So he saw his visit to Rome as imperative: *'I **must** visit Rome'* (Acts 19:21). But there was a barrier.

When Christianity first reached Rome it was seen and treated as a variant of being Jewish, but had begun to make considerable headway. It was perhaps because of the fierce arguments and tensions that Christianity was causing in the Jewish sectors of the city that in AD 49 the Emperor Claudius expelled all Jews from Rome. That would have prevented Paul from going to Rome until after Claudius' death in AD 54, and might explain why he spent longer than usual in Corinth and Ephesus, and talked of being *prevented* and *hindered* from coming to Rome (Romans 1:13, 15:22). Despite that temporary block, Paul's passion as the Apostle to the Gentiles to visit the centre point of the Empire, the place that most represented *the ends of the earth,* kept burning (Acts 13:47).

Despite the Jewish ejection, the gospel continued to expand in Rome and their *faith* (was) *being reported all over the world* (Romans 1:8; 16:16). But in AD 64, under the Emperor Nero, those overcrowded tenements had caught fire and he badly needed a scapegoat to take the blame for what many thought was an attempt to make more land available for his grandiose building projects. The scapegoats were the Christians. The first Roman persecution of Christianity started as a piece of political sleight of hand by Nero, and although it did not become an official policy until much later, it was a practice much used then and under subsequent emperors.

It is in the shadow of Nero's unpredictable rages that 2 Timothy shows Paul arrested, on trial, and facing an uncertain future. Under a paranoid tyrant, capable of requiring people to worship him as god, to claim loyalty to a higher God, judge, and king (4:1,8) would have been a provocative act. It should not be too surprising that a number of Christians were beginning to find their allegiance to Paul in his imprisonment severely tested (1:15).

EPHESUS

The erratic whim of the Emperor met its match in the vast and bureaucratic empire, and in the provinces the more regular power of Roman law held sway. Timothy does not appear to have been in imminent danger of arrest or imprisonment. Rather, the wealth, pluralism and importance of Ephesus seem to have been beguiling the Christians in quite a different direction.

It was the administrative centre for the province, and its large harbour and good road system provided constant traffic and trade. It was almost inevitable that a new idea would come to Ephesus sooner or later, and the vast cult to Diana gave an all-embracing welcome to a range of spiritualities and mysticisms. The temple to Diana of the Ephesians was not merely huge, decadent and corrupt, it was one of the two main centres of economic and political power in the city. The other was the cult of worshipping the Roman Empire, symbolised in its Emperor. Without allegiance to one of those two (and the norm would have been to visit and give to the temples of both Diana and Caesar) it would have been impossible to find a reasonable place in society. This was where deals were made and business done, friendships forged and bribes offered.

Ephesus was about three things: trade, the erotic cult of Diana and the armed might of the Empire. Christians who were determined to avoid the attractions of pagan worship and to be obedient over money, sex and power found themselves forever on the outside, excluded and ignored.

The problems encountered in the church in 1 Timothy reflect the difficulties of trying to be a pure church in a decadent but religious culture. A fascination with mysticism (1 Timothy 1:3–4), asceticism (1 Timothy 4:3) and minute points of Jewish laws (1 Timothy 1:7) appeared alongside extravagance (1 Timothy 2:9) and explicit paganism (1 Timothy 4:1). In Revelation, Ephesus is applauded as a church which has tackled its fascination with a range of error (Revelation 2:2,6). In those circumstances it is probably impossible to pin down the error being addressed in 2 Timothy with great precision. But undoubtedly the combination of religious and economic power in the city made life increasingly difficult for a believer the more he or she stood out for the uniqueness of the gospel. The false teaching seems to have had the impact of easing the Christians back into an accepted place in a tolerant society, because it reduced its larger truth claims (see below on 2:18).

The two cities represent two different pulls on the Christians – Rome threatened, and Ephesus wooed. In both cases a believer who stood out was isolated, and the believer who compromised was welcomed as a sensible person who did not take religion too seriously. By refusing to stand on principle, Paul might have his freedom and Timothy might reclaim some Christians who thought he was too hard line. It was, and remains, hard to resist that double call.

6

The themes of the letter

A letter like 2 Timothy is not supposed to yield all its secrets at once (2:7), so at the outset it might be helpful to highlight some of the main themes that Paul will consider. In that way even a reader unfamiliar with the letter can pick up some connections and allusions from the beginning.

SUFFERING FOR THE GOSPEL

This is a theme which is obvious even on first reading. Paul is in prison, and he explains it is because he is a faithful gospel teacher (1:11–12); he expects Timothy to show similar resilience (2:3), and to encourage others to follow the same path (2:2).

Paul's suffering seems to have two causes: the opposition of the state, and the opposition of the churches (see **Being ashamed** below). The two seem to be connected, in that Christians who could have helped Paul are refusing to do so (4:16). Paul wants them to remain loyal to his gospel ministry, but then they will share the experience of the same double-headed opposition.

FALSE TEACHING

There is clearly some false version of Christianity being spread in Ephesus, and it is causing Paul considerable anxiety. Because of its content it will spread (2:17, see **Past, present and future** below), and the only successful way of combating false teaching is through the preparation for a succession of good Bible teachers in the future (2:1–2, see **Ministry** below).

PAST, PRESENT AND FUTURE

The only insight into the nature of the false teaching troubling Timothy's church is that *they say that the resurrection has already taken place, and they destroy the faith of some* (2:18). The comments on that section show how this treatment could infect the churches and sap the morale of people of Timothy's calibre. Paul's answer is to flood the letter, literally from start to finish (1:1; 4:18) with positive teaching and motivation about God's plan for the future, both in terms of gospel growth and the return of Jesus Christ. His reply is sketched out in the comments on 1:1–2, and is a major running motif of the whole letter.

MINISTRY

Timothy is the first line of defence in Ephesus, and much of Paul's work is concerned to drive him back to his work of evangelism and teaching. He is also to ensure that when he leaves Ephesus there are equipped teachers for the church's future.

This means that the first line of application throughout this exposition will be about church leadership. Take that in its widest sense to mean Bible study leadership and Sunday School and the lessons will still apply. The last words of the letter imply that everyone in the church is to know what it contains (4:22, the Greek work for *you* is plural), even if all we can do for our leaders is pray for them as they face pressure.

BEING ASHAMED

The greatest pressure that Timothy faced was to *be ashamed* of the gospel, its Lord, and Paul, his prisoner. As the theme becomes clearer the issue becomes not one of mere embarrassment, but that in Timothy's culture and to some extent in Timothy's church, he would pay a price for being loyal to Paul's teaching. Many Christians today live in cultures where loyalty to the gospel is a matter of ridicule or even illegality, and the letter is for those times and places. Sadly, some belong to denominations like that, and this letter is for them, too.

7

The shape of the letter

The way Paul writes 2 Timothy is not difficult to grasp. There is a clear line of argument from the opening of the letter proper in 1:3 through to 3:17, and Paul makes frequent use of parallel examples, some good (1:16–18), some bad (1:15), or drawn from the Old Testament (3:8), Jesus (2:8), Timothy's experience (1:5) and Paul himself (3:10).

These parallels are clearly part of Paul's argument, as he seeks to draw Timothy away from unfruitful ways of thinking and behaving into more positive patterns. The personal contrasts are highlighted by phrases such as *You then* (2:1), or *You, however* (3:10), or placing one illustration up against a direct application to Timothy, such as *What you heard from me* (in the previous few verses) *keep as the pattern of sound teaching* (1:13).

Paul knows that patterns of thought and habits of Christian behaviour are caught as well as taught, which is why he reminds Timothy to *Flee the evil desires of youth, and pursue righteousness, faith, love and peace, along with those who call on the Lord out of a pure heart* (2:22). As Timothy moves out of circles with bad practices, and moves into circles with good ones, so he in turn will become a good model for younger Christians who are potential leaders (2:2).

Once Paul's way of writing is noticed, the structure becomes much clearer, and apparent asides prove to be clear illustrations of the truth he is communicating.

There is one apparent exception to the smooth flow of the letter. At 4:1 Paul seems suddenly to change direction and mood, and almost to write a different kind of letter.

But a sudden change of mood like that is actually far from uncommon in New Testament letters (for example, Romans 12:1, 2 Corinthians 10:1, Philippians 4:1). There is a similar moment in 2 Peter 3:1, which is so sudden that some have misread it as the start of a new letter. Such sharp breaks are literary marks that the author is going to apply the lessons he is writing about, in one last and much more personal vein. Both 2 Peter and 2 Timothy share the pattern of an apostle calling an erring church back into line, and aware that as they near the end of their ministry they see dark clouds on the horizon. So perhaps it is better to imagine this as a moment when both author and readers should pause, take a deep breath, and engage with the heart of the letter.

Chapter Four does have an independent structure to the rest of the letter, and in Section 25 below, 4:1 will be looked at as an introduction to 4:2–18.

8

A genuine letter?

Most contemporary scholars do not think Paul wrote 2 Timothy, nor indeed any of the three so-called Pastoral Letters, but this issue is not closed. All the major commentaries have long sections on the question of authorship, and the reader who wants to investigate further needs to consult several of them. The concerns seem to centre on four issues, and all we can do here is indicate the kind of approach that this exposition takes and the lines of enquiry that seem most fruitful.

THE PASTORAL LETTERS?

Titus, 1 and 2 Timothy have been bracketed together since the early days of the church compiling the New Testament. They have been known collectively as 'The Pastoral Letters' for about two hundred and fifty years, and they show similarities of style that bind them together and mark them off from other New Testament letters. One result of this bracketing has been to characterise all three of them as concerned with church order, and to think of them as late, institutionally concerned letters which could not have been written by the creative Paul.

That is a misreading of all three letters, none of which has those concerns and whose passions lie elsewhere. What that misreading does for 2 Timothy is to hide the fact that it is different to 1 Timothy and Titus in a number of respects, and that the letter to which it bears greatest similarity is the unquestionably authentic Philippians. There are echoes of concern, language, and also of the style where Paul draws constant comparisons, good and bad, from others, himself, scripture and Jesus.

So 2 Timothy has similarities with both an undoubted letter by Paul and 1 Timothy and Titus. Losing the title 'Pastoral' and uncoupling these letters might prove beneficial for all three.

CHRONOLOGY

The difficulty for defending the traditional authorship is that there is no match between Paul's circumstances in the letter and his known circumstances in life. Acts finishes with him under house arrest, with considerable freedom and no time pressure. In 2 Timothy he is once more chained and anxious. The trial (4:16–17) points to Paul being in Rome. Timothy was in Ephesus when 1 Timothy was written (1 Timothy 1:3), and the continuity of people Paul mentions means that he was still there (1 Timothy 1:20, 2 Timothy 2:17). In addition Paul says Timothy knows that Onesiphorus helped him in Ephesus (1:18), and Timothy is to greet the man's household (4:19). It is a reasonable assumption that he helped Paul in the city where he lived. So although Paul does not state that Timothy was in Ephesus, the circumstantial evidence points clearly to Timothy being there.

There is a strong tradition which states that Paul was freed after his imprisonment in Acts and conducted more church planting work, leaving Titus in Crete (Titus 1:5) and Timothy in Ephesus. He headed west to Spain, and then back into the Mediterranean basin, was then rearrested (in Troas (4:13)?) and brought to trial in Rome under the much more savage persecutions of Nero's latter reign. Shortly after this letter he was beheaded and buried with Peter on the Ostian Way beyond Rome. The tradition is found in Clement's first letter, written in the mid-nineties *(1 Clement 5)* and in the later *Eusebius* (AD 325) who refers to an early source (*History of the Church,* 2:25).

Those who are convinced that Paul wrote 2 Timothy find that a satisfying description; those who think someone else wrote it in his name see that tradition as one which grew up around the letter to explain it. The argument can cut both ways and decisions on authorship have to be made on other grounds. However, there is no rival interpretation available for what happened at the end of Paul's life. If that tradition is untrue and 2 Timothy is not by Paul then we know nothing at all about its origins.

LANGUAGE

There have been countless attempts to calculate the sentence length and vocabulary of Paul's letters and compare them with the few unquestionably genuine letters. For the Pastorals they usually point to some dissimilarity for 2 Timothy and considerably more for 1 Timothy and Titus.

Raw data needs interpreting, and there have been many such interpretations beyond the obvious one that these letters are not by Paul. The most usual has been to say that Paul used some secretarial help, whether Luke or someone else, and the variations in style are accounted for by that. That is a persuasive argument, because Paul's opportunities for writing, certainly in the constricted circumstances of 2 Timothy, would have been more limited and outside help would have been needed, and it was his practice elsewhere to use secretaries (Romans 16:22, Galatians 6:11).

Another more recent explanation is that writers in the ancient world would deliberately adopt a particular 'voice' or recognisable style to match the mood and intent of the piece they were writing. That is still common practice today, of course, but it was then a much more recognised feature of accomplished writing. What scholars may have missed in the past, it is now being suggested, is that we should not expect Paul's letters to have similar vocabulary, sentence length or style because they were drafted according to differing methods of writing. A passionate letter like 2 Timothy was expected to have a markedly different feel to a cooler letter like Titus. That was good style and persuasive writing. So perhaps the computer analyses are less weighty than has been thought.

PSEUDEPIGRAPHY

It was common in the ancient world for letters and speeches to be written in the style and name of a dead hero, and it was a feature of religious writing too. One of the explanations for the differences in style of the Pastoral letters is that they are an example of an anonymous person writing in the character of Paul, to preserve elements of his teaching (that is, Pseudepigraphy). This was not forgery, it is said, because it was a recognised way of recording otherwise lost tradition, and no-one was intended to be fooled by it.

Four major obstacles stand in the way of the acceptance of this explanation.

The first is that when the early church was deciding what to recognise as authentic apostolic writing they did not use this criterion. Pieces were either authentic or inauthentic. There is no record of an argument that said 'This is not by Paul, but it is valid pseudepigraphy and therefore can be included'. The criterion does not seem to have existed.

Second, the authentic Pauline letters recognise that there are fakes going around and attempt to stop them (2 Thessalonians 2:2). So there would have been a definite interest in, and measurements for, authenticity.

Third, all the examples of pseudepigraphy appear well after the death of the hero – from people like Abraham or Moses – where there could have been no possibility of confusion over authorship. There is apparently no evidence of pseudepigraphy being written within the living memory of the person who had died, and written with no intention to deceive. That is even true for the literary genre called 'Testament', a style of farewell letter from senior to junior leaders. Not only is there no evidence of a Testament being written so close to the death of the hero, there is the further problem that a farewell letter would contain fairly predictable elements whether it is genuine or a fiction.

Fourth, there is the volume of material in 2 Timothy that relates to the personal circumstances of Paul or Timothy, occurring in almost every section, and frequently being the hinge point of an argument. To skim the surface, Paul writes of his present circumstances (1:12; 2:9) and uses himself as an example (1:8,12; 2:2,3,9; 3:10 etc.). He is intimately familiar with Timothy's family (1:5), spiritual upbringing (3:15), and ministry (1:6), and he knows both the positive (1:16; 4:19) and negative (2:17–18) members of Timothy's current experience. Timothy, in his turn, is to remember what he saw (3:10–11) and heard (2:2) from Paul, and to build on their network of mutual friends (4:19–21). The whole of Chapter Four depends for its force on the reality of the danger inherent in Paul's imprisonment and the necessity of Timothy's coming to Rome (4:11–13).

Unless there could be clear evidence that this amount of personal material was accepted by the early Christians as a stylistic form to be used in pseudepigraphy, then the weight of evidence must lie the other way around. From the earliest times, the intimate side of this letter was taken as the natural content of a letter between two affectionate and separated friends. That is still how it reads most naturally today. The alternative is that what was written was a piece of calculated deception, and it should be treated as such. That the early Christians did not do so speaks strongly in its favour.

THE RING OF TRUTH

For myself, I am convinced that Paul wrote all three of the Pastorals, partly because when one inhabits them for a long period of time they seem increasingly genuine in passion and tone, and partly because of the implausibility of the alternatives. My first reason is subjective, and other people who have spent far longer in the study have concluded otherwise, but there is a transparent honesty about Paul's concerns in 2 Timothy, and such a great concern for authenticity in the teaching ministry, that it would be difficult to conclude of its being written as a pious fiction. There is too much energy and concern in it. For the alternatives, one has to read the arguments and weigh them. I cannot see the appropriate practice of pseudepigraphy accepted in the early church, nor existence of the theological giants necessary to write these works anonymously.

Reading 2 Timothy Today (2)

9

The promise of life

1:1–2

The opening few words of most of the letters in the New Testament have a family likeness. Like the normal correspondence of their day they mention both the sender and recipient, perhaps as a simple reminder to the letter-carrier, and they typically adapt that greeting with some Christian words. Here, Paul wishes Timothy *Grace, mercy and peace.* So the letter opens and closes on the note of *grace* (4:22). He reminds Timothy that he is a *dear son,* which sets the tone for the encouragement Paul will give. Paul says that he is *an apostle of Christ Jesus by the will of God,* which gives such a grand authority to the gospel he has passed on that Timothy should be willing to pay any price to protect it. So affection and authority mark the way Paul will strengthen this church leader. Although he is writing a personal letter to one man it is not private, because the final words, *Grace be with you,* are plural. Church leadership needs to be understood by the church membership.

Often, Paul will include in the opening greeting some indication of a major theme he is going to address in the letter (for instance Romans opens with a declaration of the gospel and Paul's apostleship, 1 Corinthians opens with a reminder that Christians are to be both holy and united, and so on). In the opening words of 2 Timothy, the key phrase is *the promise of life.*

LIFE AND DEATH

Life is God's gift to us. He *breathed ... the breath of life* into Adam (Genesis 2:7), and gave unrestricted access to *the tree of life* (Genesis 2:9) on the simple but crucial condition that he was obeyed. The essence of the matter was that humans should trust God over what is right and wrong, and not set up an alternative moral system. That was crystallised in *the tree of the knowledge of good and evil* (Genesis 2:17), from which they were commanded not to eat. As long as they obeyed God he was the ultimate ruler, but if they decided to take the fruit they would be trying to rule the garden independently of him, and they would pay the penalty.

They did, of course, take the fruit and they did pay the penalty. God had warned that *when you eat of it you will surely die* (Genesis 2:17), and they heard God's solemn judgment that mankind will *return to the ground, since from it you were taken; for dust you are and to dust you will return* (Genesis 3:19). They were banished from the garden with its tree of life, because Adam *must not be allowed to reach out his hand and take also from the tree of life and eat, and live forever* (Genesis 3:22). Instead they face death.

The quite remarkable thing is that the Bible does not stop there. God places a death penalty over the human race, but does not implement it straight away. Instead, he helps them produce the next generation (Genesis 4:1). God has a rescue plan in mind. Although he *cursed* the serpent (3:14) and the ground (3:17) he does not curse the people but promises a deliverer for them. From the larger Bible picture we recognise that God's curse on rebellious human beings will only ultimately be announced on judgment day, when Jesus says *Depart from me, you who are cursed, into the eternal fire prepared for the devil and his angels* (Matthew 25:41). The ultimate curse still lies ahead of the entire human race.

With one important exception: *Christ redeemed us from the curse of the law by becoming a curse for us* (Galatians 3:13), which means that he has already faced that dreadful day of judgment on our behalf, and in his death he took the penalty for our rebellion. The reason that God did not execute judgment on Adam and Eve was so that he could take the penalty on himself. Quite literally, Jesus died on our behalf.

THE PROMISE OF LIFE

Having taken that penalty for us, Jesus was rewarded with being raised from the dead. At various points in the Old Testament it was becoming clear that there was an expectation of life beyond the grave. Hebrews tells us that *Abraham reasoned that God could raise the dead* (Hebrews 11:19), which was why he was willing to sacrifice Isaac – the son God had promised would produce a huge nation of descendants. Notice how Abraham says to his servant that *we* (Abraham and Isaac) *will worship* (that is, sacrifice Isaac) *and then we* (the pair of them) *will come back to you* (Genesis 22:5). Psalm 23 reflects a frequent pattern in the Psalms – the king will *walk through the valley of the shadow of death,* and yet subsequently live and reign forever (Psalm 23:4,6). Job has the odd hope that *after my skin has been destroyed yet in my flesh I will see God* (Job 19:26). Such passages are individually debatable, but the cumulative effect of these and many others is that there were the beginnings of the hope of resurrection.

Its clearest expression is in Daniel 12, where the prophet was told of a time when *Multitudes who sleep in the dust of the earth will awake: some to everlasting life, others to shame and everlasting contempt* (Daniel 12:2). That is the promise of life in its clearest form: that at some future stage there will be what the New Testament came to call the Resurrection, and it will be followed by judgment, either to life or to contempt, meaning to death. The New Testament clarifies this on one important point: the judge on resurrection day will be Jesus, appointed by God for this task because he has already been raised from the dead and installed as universal Lord. God *has set a day when he will judge the world with justice by the man he has appointed. He has given proof of this to all men by raising him from the dead* (Acts 17:31). The proof lies in the fact that resurrection and judgment belong together, and Resurrection Day is Judgment Day. Jesus' being raised from the dead proves that Resurrection Day is certain because it has already begun. But because Jesus died for us, it is possible for Resurrection Day to be Salvation Day for anyone who believes in him.

So when Paul writes here of being *an apostle of Christ Jesus by the will of God, according to the promise of life that is in Christ Jesus* (1:1) he means quite precisely that his message and ministry are to be seen in a direct line with everything God has done in human history to fulfil his promise up to that point. Paul's ministry as an apostle is to announce the resurrection of Jesus (1:10–11), and that the same message is to be Timothy's and ours until Christ's return and the general resurrection and final judgment takes place (4:1–2).

Paul will keep returning to this theme throughout the letter. It will act as an encouragement (4:8) and a warning (4:14); it gives Timothy the largest possible picture of the consequences of his ministry, explaining both its eternal significance (4:1–2) and its temporary setbacks (3:1); it is to be a spur to Timothy himself, his fellow Christians, and all of us who believe him (2:11). The theme of being a Christian in the 'Last Days' (or 'eschatology', from the Greek word *eschaton,* the End), and the application of those lessons to a Christian leader, is the heart of 2 Timothy.

THE THREAT TO THE PROMISE

The reason for this insistence lies in the few hints Paul gives at the error that was being smuggled into the church in Ephesus, and which was causing Timothy such heartache. There are general references to deception (3:13) and opposing the truth (3:8), and the fact that there was evident if short term success for these people (4:3). But the single verse which mentions their doctrinal error is 2:18: *They say that the resurrection has already taken place, and they destroy the faith of some.* It is an error over eschatology.

Quite clearly they cannot be stating that Jesus' resurrection has taken place, because Paul would affirm that. They are saying that in some way Resurrection Day has taken place. It is impossible to be precise over how they managed to say this, but two cases suggest themselves. One would be the route of radically redefining what *the resurrection* meant. Perhaps in the light of contemporary Greek philosophies they considered the body unimportant and only the soul of any significance. In that case the idea of a Resurrection Day was absurd and unnecessary. Every Christian is as fully resurrected as she or he will ever be, and when we die we will simply go to heaven for eternity while our bodies go back to the dust from where they came.

This would undoubtedly *destroy the faith of some,* just as every subsequent attempt to redefine such issues has done. The return of Christ, the general resurrection, and Christ's judgment over people are all lost in such reinterpretation. Every element in the New Testament that has the return of Christ as its mainspring will have to be re-interpreted as powerful poetry and myth, but either mistaken in what it teaches, or mistakenly read as if there were a future plan of God. In other words, it would have to undergo a process that its leading advocates in the last century called 'demythologising', re-reading the 'mythical' elements of New Testament Christianity.

Perhaps because the impact of that movement was so widespread, particularly among the churches in Western countries, we are better placed than almost any Christians since Timothy to gauge the impact of such teaching. The morning I wrote these sentences another survey was published indicating that attendance at churches across Britain has declined steeply once more. After fifty years during which the future leaders of churches have been taught in their colleges that *the resurrection* (or, at least, as much of it as was ever going to occur) *has already happened,* and that the natural meaning of such words must be changed to something more credible to the mind of contemporary society, it would be a fool who denied that the impact of such teaching has been to destroy the faith of a great many.

Another, equally possible, way of reading 2:18 would be to take it in a much more positive and upbeat way. These people really did imagine that Resurrection Day had occurred and all the blessings that were going to come to them on that day were theirs already. Sinless and eternally healthy, co-reigning with Christ in glory, they have a message of great success and ease. They would have great problems understanding Paul's view on suffering as an apostle (1:12) because such experiences should have no place in the life of a risen Christian.

It is clear to see how this might *destroy the faith of some.* Once again there is a reinterpretation, but this time it is not so much a reinterpretation of doctrine as of reality. People would be called to live as if what they could see with their eyes and know in their hearts were plainly not so. Such over-enthusiasm has an inevitable backwash as gullible Christians discover that despite their best efforts, sin and sickness are still a reality. The reinterpretation has not worked. Once bitten, and twice shy, such people do not necessarily return to the real message – they all too easily slide off into cynicism which will never listen to the claims of Christ again. The result would be a generation of hardened ex-Christians, impervious to real Christianity. Once again, faith is destroyed.

Those two options are not the only ones, to be sure, and the best a modern reader can do is to try to sketch in the outlines of what have might have been said to make Paul respond as he did.

In these opening words, then, Paul has raised an issue that will concentrate his thinking throughout the letter, and which is painfully relevant to anyone who is a member of a church today. It is a rare pastor who has not seen members disappear from the fringes of the church, either because *the promise of life that is in Christ Jesus* is too crude and naive for today's multi-culturalists, or that it is too deferred and unreal for today's instant consumers. Keeping the focus clearly on the reality of the *life* that Christ has won for us, and that it comes to us in the form of a *promise* is no easy task, as Timothy had already found out.

STUDY, DISCUSSION AND PRAYER

1. How much of a place does Jesus' return have in your thinking?

2. How might saying that 'the resurrection has already happened' destroy your faith?

3. Pray for anyone you know who believes, or teaches, false ideas about the resurrection.

4. Pray for anyone you know who has started to believe false teaching about the resurrection, or has left your church claiming either that 'the teaching is too narrow' or that 'the services are not experiencing the fullness of God's resurrection power'.

10

The next link in the chain

1:3–7

Paul's opening words are a strange way to begin a letter to someone Paul has known since the younger man's first days as a Christian, has trained in church leadership, and has deployed in countless difficult pastoral situations (1 Corinthians 16:10–11, 1 Timothy 1:3). We have an impressive model in Paul's praying, but do we have any clues here as to what he is praying so earnestly about? Why does he remind Timothy of their respective family trees? Why is Timothy so tearful – and why would Paul have tolerated such a spineless individual?

TAKING HIS TURN

Paul is clearly making a point about a responsibility being handed on through the generations, much as a relay runner hands on a baton. He has received the baton from his Jewish *forefathers*, and he has continued to serve God. The reference to his *clear conscience* is probably because he is currently on trial for holding to a new and illegal religion. Paul wants it known that faith in *Christ Jesus our Lord* (1:2) is not a new heresy because Jesus the Messiah is the fulfilment of Jewish hopes. However much the Lord Caesar might have seen it as treason, Paul stands at the end of a long line of believers in God's promises.

So too does Timothy. As Lois and Eunice were Jewish then he also has roots that go back to Abraham, and he was nurtured in that faith from childhood (3:15). At some point all three of them have been converted, his mother and grandmother *first*, and Timothy subsequently, and if he was converted under Paul on that first missionary journey, then that little word *son* (1:2) deliberately ties Timothy into both the family trees that Paul has sketched.

Perhaps this stress on belonging occurs so close to the opening of the letter as a clue to what will follow. Paul is concerned that Timothy will drop the baton as it is placed into his hand. He has not dropped it yet, for Paul knows that his faith is *sincere*, but he knows too that Timothy is exceedingly anxious about the future. Timothy's famous *tears* are easily understood at this point if a little imagination is used. If those tears were at his last meeting with Paul, then various stresses were bearing on him. He knew that he would probably never see Paul again, and that alone would have caused him to be emotional. He knew that Paul was being taken into a deeply unpleasant prison regime where the end would be possibly torture, probably death (Acts 20:22–24), and that this heralded the beginning of a new program of terror against the churches, which would involve him as well. In addition he was facing the prospect of leading a dwindling church where his leadership was being questioned and where the opposition Paul had hoped to discipline had returned with renewed strength (1 Timothy 1:20, 2 Timothy 2:17–18). Timothy would have to have been a remarkable man not to feel enormous anxiety at the future. He faced the prospect of carrying the apostolic message to a new generation just as the church decided it did not want it and the state decided that it would eliminate it.

That combined weight of personal responsibility, frustration, fear and grief would make any man shudder, and Timothy was no weakling to express that in *tears*, as did others (Acts 20:36–38). Deep in his cell Paul shared that anxiety which kept him awake as much as it did Timothy. Would even Timothy have the personal resources to cope with this massive burden? Paul prayed *constantly* for Timothy, and decided that for the sake of his peace of mind, and to encourage the younger man, he would call him across to Rome. In that way he would be able to assure the church at Ephesus that his imprisonment did not mean the end of the gospel. In fact, despite a hostile state and a worldly church, the reverse was the case, and might even result in the church growing as it never had before (Philippians 1:12).

POWER, LOVE AND SELF-DISCIPLINE

As Timothy faced such an uncertain and worrying future, he needed to be reminded of the resources that God had given him. The Holy Spirit (the word 'Spirit' should probably have capital letters here) has been given to Timothy as to all Christians, and part of his work is to equip us for the ministries God has given us. It is not clear here whether Paul's *laying on of ... hands* refers to Timothy's conversion or his commissioning as a church leader, and in any case makes little difference. Paul is certain that every Christian has received the Holy Spirit by definition (1 Corinthians 12:3), and also that Timothy has a particular gift from God (1 Timothy 4:14) as, by inference, have other, future, leaders. But Timothy's cowardice, whether as a Christian or more particularly as a Christian leader, is not an appropriate way for a Spirit-filled person to behave. Whether he dressed it up as prudence or tact, or just knew he was a coward and couldn't see any way out of it, Timothy was not behaving well.

Instead he should be acting in line with three aspects of the work of the Holy Spirit. These are not plucked out at random, but chosen by Paul as particularly important for a pastor tempted to duck out of ministerial responsibilities. It is clear that Paul had not laid hands on Timothy as the next apostle, but as a delegate of an apostle. After the replacement of Judas by Matthias (Acts 1:12–26) and the day of Pentecost, there was never again a need to fill in a vacancy in the apostles' ranks. James died (Acts 12:2) and was not replaced because the apostles have a once-for-all authority in the church. What they said then has an abiding authority today, and they need no continuing successor because they still exercise that same authority in their writings. In one sense every minister today stands in the shoes of Timothy, hearing the commands and charges of an apostle, commissioning and challenging us to wholehearted service. There are no authoritative apostles today, but there are millions of Timothys. He may well be the New Testament character with whom many of us should identify most readily. Since we all stand with Paul's hands on our shoulders, and since we are all filled with the same Holy Spirit, we can read these words as a threefold promise for our ministries too.

Power is the aspect we notice first, and in our strong-minded age it is the one we should have recommended first. What would be more appropriate than for Timothy to meet his troublemakers face to face, confront them and drive them out of the church! But of course Paul does not mean anything like that, and our ideas of what *power* should look like in church leaders is often merely a distressing and poor reflection of our surrounding culture. As Paul will show in the next section, the power he has in mind is one that will enable Timothy to continue *suffering for the gospel, by the power of God* (1:8). Power means nothing more dynamic than that Timothy will continue in ministry. But as any pastor will testify, it is a sovereign work of God to keep anyone in the hard task of church leadership.

Timothy's ability to *love* was being sorely tested by the presence of aggressive false teachers, gullible Christians and treacherous leaders (1:15; 4:3–4). Any Christian leader can love the flock when it is well-mannered, eager to learn, and obedient. But how can we love the flock when they are rude, ignorant and wilful – in short, *without love* (3:3)?

Again, it will be the witness of any Christian leader that a Christian without love can inflict the most painful wounds – and yet, the task is still to love back. How is Timothy to do such an impossible task? Only by asking for the resources of the Holy Spirit.

Those self same forces which defied Timothy to love them were presumably the reason that Timothy was tempted to fall down on the job. Depressed and demoralised, feeling that the concern for the churches lay on his shoulders alone (cf Philippians 2:20), Timothy was perhaps growing slack. Like the soldier running away from the fight, like the athlete cutting corners, and like the farmer who lets the farm look after itself (2:3–6), Timothy was finding it hard to be motivated to continue. The answer, again, is the work of the Holy Spirit, who will equip him to stop acting in a cowardly way, and to turn from self-pity to *self-discipline.*

STUDY, DISCUSSION AND PRAYER

1. Identify something you need to pray about in the areas of:
    - Timidity/cowardice
    - Power
    - Love
    - Self control

2. What have you learned about praying for the leaders in your church?

3. Pray!

11

Suffering for the gospel of grace

1:8-12

This section is one of the hardest in the whole of 2 Timothy. Its difficulty does not lie in its being obscure or complicated. It is, for the most part, crystal clear (but see below on 1:12). The difficulty is that its assumptions and teaching run in such opposition to much contemporary Christianity that many will simply not wish to tune into its message. In the areas of our expectations of success in church life, of self fulfilment in our private life, and of our preference for easy truths in our intellectual life, Paul will challenge us with suffering, holiness and the doctrine of predestination.

THE PRICE OF THE GOSPEL – SUFFERING WITH PAUL AND JESUS

Paul and Timothy lived in what is sometimes called a 'shame culture'. Relationships were governed by a complex pattern of obligations and duties, favours that needed to be repaid and status marks that needed to be preserved. Some people were born into, or moved into, higher status than others, and each rung on the ladder, up or down, was precisely calculated. Being lower down the ladder was not a good place to be.

Paul had previously exposed the danger of Christians playing those status games with one another (2 Corinthians

11:16–33). Even if the society of their time used exaggerated rules, the same patterns and dangers are easily visible in our society, and in our churches today. Some congregations have a higher status than others, whether because of their size (small defers to large), resources (poor defers to wealthy) or membership (older defers to younger, especially if the younger are students). Of course, no-one would ever refer to 'high-status churches' because that would be too crude; the term we use instead is 'strategic'.

Paul found himself in a low-status position, in a deeply status driven culture. Prison then, even more than now, was a place of dishonour and shame. It was, to their eyes, definitely not strategic. No matter that Paul had not finished his trial, that the verdict had not yet been given and the sentence still lay in the future; the mere fact of being in prison made him an object of pity and derision. Still worse, the message he was proclaiming which had landed him in prison was itself about an object of shame: a cross. Curiously, he was even willing to boast about this object of shame (Galatians 6:14), because to him it was the *power of God and the wisdom of God* (1 Corinthians 1:24). To his persecutors, Paul was not only living in the gutter, but he had dragged his God down there with him.

Those persecutors were not only the officials, lawyers and zealots who had hounded him around the Mediterranean, but some of the very people he had converted, discipled and placed in leadership but who had subsequently found that allegiance to such a man was too high a price to pay. He was, simply, an embarrassment. And slowly people began to distance themselves from him.

Paul's plea is therefore both poignant and devastating: *Do not be ashamed to testify about our Lord, or ashamed of me, his prisoner.* It is poignant because he is obviously feeling isolated and unsupported, and fearful of losing Timothy's loyalty. It is devastating because what is at stake is far more than his loneliness or a valued friendship. If Timothy edges away from Paul out of embarrassment, he will find that he has edged away from Jesus too. Paul's imprisonment is so closely identified with Jesus' ministry that they cannot, at one level, be untangled, and to break faith with Paul is to break faith with his Lord.

We do not have the same embarrassment about Paul, who is no longer in prison but safely in his tomb. It is possible to think of his incarceration without a shudder. But the mention of his name still evokes a strong, and largely negative, reaction in many churches. Jesus is adored and loved, quite rightly. But Paul is blamed for all the ills of the church: it is alleged he turned a gentle message of love into a doctrinaire system; he turned Jesus from a hero to be admired into a Lord to be submitted to; he turned a Jewish carpenter into a figure from an entirely different religion. In key recent debates, whether over women's ordination, sexuality, or dialogue with other faiths, Paul has continually been represented as the one who is time-bound and who has not thought through the implications of his faith on issues such as slavery or marriage. Jesus, of course, is said to represent a deeper, simpler, faith, but Paul is locked-in as a man of his time.

For all that those are complex issues, Paul is absolutely insistent: to be ashamed of him is inevitably to be ashamed of Jesus, and to be loyal to Jesus means being loyal to Paul, and therefore to engage in the same costly *suffering* for the gospel. Here, perhaps, we are most ashamed of him, because contemporary Christianity does not want to *join with me in suffering for the gospel.* We like our ease and relaxation, and we expect church to fit in the part of our life called 'leisure'; the task of the church is to teach us how to have successful marriages, families, jobs and retirements, how to order our time to be healthy and holy, be generous and have a lovely home. Paul, cold, hungry and isolated is an embarrassment. But then, so is a cross.

THE CHALLENGE OF THE GOSPEL – THE CALLING TO A HOLY LIFE

Living wholeheartedly as a Christian, standing out from our prevailing culture and being seen to be different, is hard, which is why Paul tells Timothy that he will not be able to do it on his own but that he will suffer with Paul *by the power of God.* This was where Paul was heading when he raised *power* in verse 7. God's power is not necessarily to be seen in ways we might think obvious, like many converts or large congregations, but it is to be seen in an individual, Timothy, staying loyal to Paul and Jesus against the full force of a contemptuous culture and church. The difficulty of Timothy's doing that unaided is so great, in Paul's eyes, that it can only be attributed to God's power if he succeeds.

Paul goes further, and reminds Timothy of where he stands as a Christian: he has been saved from the destiny that his society will face, and he has been *called ... to a holy life* in clear distinction to his society's values. 'Calling', in the Bible, does not refer to one's occupation, and certainly not to a few Christians who are 'called' into particular high status professions such as medicine or education, or being clergy or missionaries. We distort an important Bible truth with that kind of thinking, which is that God has *called* every Christian, meaning he has converted them, and he has *called* every Christian *to a holy life.*

Standing out from the crowd as a Christian, and being known for being loyal to Jesus, is a price that every Christian is expected to pay. Christianity is not a status religion, and it knows nothing of elites. Everyone, not a few, has been called, and everyone, not a few, has been called to be holy.

THE GLORY OF THE GOSPEL – A GOD OVER TIME

Paul continues, teaching various aspects of what theologians call the doctrine of Predestination, which states that God controls and rules the future, and has decided on that future in detail from way back in eternity. It is a doctrine which many Christians over time have dismissed as impossible, because the future is unknowable by definition, even to God, offensive, because it removes human responsibility from the equation, or unintelligible, because it leaves us with a series of unanswered and seemingly unanswerable questions.

Yet Paul raises this issue with Timothy here, not because he wants to have a divisive argument or a word puzzle, but because he thinks that understanding it will do him good. The message to Timothy, who was experiencing failure and anticipating worse, perhaps fearing that he had let God down, was that God had saved and called him *not because of anything we have done, but because of his own purpose and grace.* The fact that God chooses us for salvation irrespective of our own worthiness to receive it, even those of us who are ministers, is tremendous news. Those who pastor small churches, declining churches, squabbling churches or superficial churches should remember this truth as a great rock to stand on in hard times: salvation for church leaders does not depend on their effectiveness in ministry. The *purpose* of the gospel is to bring glory to God for his *grace,* his tender, loving mercy. The temptation for church leaders is to think that their own efforts will result in more praise for God, but grace is something that only God can exercise in salvation, and for which only he will take the credit.

Consider the greatness of the time-frame Paul deals with here, as he opens up the past, present and future.

God over the past

This grace was given us in Christ Jesus before the beginning of time, which is as far back in the past as one could imagine. We automatically think in time-spans, because we are creatures of time, but God's plan was formed before there was time, before there was anything we could call a 'past'. To strengthen Timothy's resolve at such a critical point, Paul reminds Timothy that the gospel he has been charged with proclaiming is no small affair, but it has a tight focus. It is only to be found *in Christ Jesus.* So Timothy can show great courage when he has grasped this again, for he will be able to stand firm when people think him trivial or narrow minded. Far from being trivial, it is God's eternal plan for the universe, and far from being narrow minded it is God's kindness to have planned it for us at all. Paul wanted Timothy to keep his eye on the single-mindedness of God, in a culture and church that was wanting to hear other truths.

God over the present

... but it (grace) has now been revealed through the appearing of our Saviour, Jesus Christ, who has brought life and immortality to light through the gospel. That wonderful word *now* does not dim with time, even though it is two thousand years since Jesus did this wonderful thing. Paul is still keeping Jesus in the centre of his frame, and in particular his saving work and therefore the cross. God's entire eternal plan hung on that cross. And because of it Jesus has brought *life and immortality to light* by his resurrection from the dead.

What distinguished Jesus' resurrection from that of Lazarus (John 11) or the others that Jesus had raised from the dead is the word *immortality* – Jesus was raised and would never die again. Not only that, his promise was that those who believed in him would share that immortality on Resurrection Day (John 11:25–26). That promise has been brought *to light,* rather as Paul has already described *the promise of life* (1:1), reminding Timothy that the full reality has not yet come, despite what some people around him are saying (2:18).

The second part of the present experience is what follows, and it is where contemporary Christianity often will not wish to go. The two thousand year-old gospel is still heard today, because Paul was appointed as its *herald ... apostle and ... teacher.* When we listen to him and his fellow apostles that same gospel is still being brought to light. In a derived sense every Christian today, and certainly every Christian leader, joins in that task (notice how Paul includes *us* [1:7,14] and calls us to *suffer with me* [1:8]). Paul's unique role is faintly echoed today when we see Christians acting as heralds, demanding that the gospel be heard and responded to, apostles, planting churches in new areas and social groups, and teachers, as they give knowledge of the truth to an ignorant world. No one today is a herald, apostle, or teacher in the same way as Paul, of course, but there are echoes of his authority as we sit under him.

Many do not want to sit under Paul's authority because of what he teaches on sexual morality or various doctrines. But many Bible-believing Christians will not want to sit under Paul's authority because of the next nine words: *that is why I am suffering as I am.* Because the gospel is such a glorious message, and because even a fragment of being a herald, apostle or teacher is a precious privilege, the temptation is to shy away from Paul's logic. But it is unavoidable. In Paul's eyes, his being in prison is an inevitable consequence of the honour of the role he has been given. It is true that Paul's apostleship involved him in suffering in a unique way (Acts 9:15–16), but his purpose in mentioning it here is to encourage Timothy to follow in his footsteps.

The logic is simple: if we are authentic Christian ministers then there will be suffering. It may not be as extreme as Paul's suffering, although there are Christian pastors in prison for their faith today, but suffering will come at some stage, for all. Timothy needs to be reminded of this of course, because of the danger of thinking that it is abnormal to suffer. His Christian subculture, much like ours, assumed that truly godly leaders will experience an automatic blessing of growth and success from God, and that leaders who find leadership tough are in the wrong job. Not at all, says Paul, God has placed me in the ministry he has, and *that is why I am suffering as I am. But I am not ashamed.*

The shame motif surfaces again, just at the point where suffering surfaces too. It may be that an individual pastor has an easy and successful ministry, but the normal pattern for most will be that they have to pay a price. This is the gospel age, which is wonderful, but that means it is the age of martyrs. But what is the reason for Paul's not being *ashamed*?

God over the future

Even this early in 2 Timothy it will be no surprise that the reason for Paul's lack of shame lies in his future perspective. He *knows* who it is who has saved and called both he and Timothy, and he has *believed* in the promises that God has made. Faith is an attitude in the present which shows that it trusts God will eventually stand by his promise for the future, however unlikely it looks here and now. Paul sees his prison cell, and the polluted churches, and yet still says *I am convinced that he is able to guard what I have entrusted to him for that day.*

Before Paul's full meaning becomes clear there is a decision to be made over what he is saying here. The problem is that the Greek text is capable of being translated in two quite different ways. It is not clear who has entrusted something to someone else: is God able to guard what God *has entrusted to* Paul, or what Paul *has entrusted to* God? If it is the former, then Paul is saying that God has entrusted Paul with the gospel and the task of proclaiming it, and that Paul trusts that God will keep the gospel true and believed until Jesus returns. If it is the latter, then Paul is saying that he has entrusted something to God (either his own life or more probably the fate of the churches) and he trusts that God will guard and protect that treasure until that day.

It is a difficult decision to make because either reading is possible, and both are defensible in the context of 2 Timothy. On the one hand, the image is of a traveller going on a journey and giving a valuable object to someone to look after. In that case, it would be odd for God to entrust something to Paul and yet still guard it. It would make more sense for Paul to entrust something valuable to God for his protection.

On the other hand, the pattern in this letter is that lessons from one person are subsequently applied to Timothy, and in verse 14 Paul tells Timothy to *Guard the good deposit that was entrusted to you.* If Paul is drawing a parallel between himself and Timothy, it only works if this verse is translated in the opposite way to the NIV: *he is able to guard what he has entrusted to me for that day.* And that must mean the gospel and its continuing impact, long after Paul's death. In my view this is the more likely meaning, but it is a difficult decision to make.

In either case, it is quite clear that Paul trusts God to *guard* what is essential for that great plan. Whether it is God guarding the gospel in order to preserve the church, or God guarding the existence of gospel ministry in the church in order to preserve the gospel, it makes little difference seen from *that day.* We live in an age that likes to call itself 'Post-Christian', and that arrogance can have a severe impact on our confidence, especially as the evidence that most denominations in the West are bleeding members and rapidly losing influence, seems to support the conclusion that Christianity's day is over. So it is worth remembering how supremely confident Paul can be. Some enthusiastic evangelists sometimes spur reluctant churches into action with the argument that 'the church is one generation from extinction'. In any one place, that is undoubtedly true. But worldwide, God has promised he will never give up on his plan, and Paul is convinced he is trustworthy.

STUDY, DISCUSSION AND PRAYER

1. Can you think of areas where you have been or might be tempted to be ashamed of Jesus, Paul or the gospel because of the personal cost to you?

2. What are the areas where you might be tempted to compromise morally?

3. Pray for the *power of God* to help you.

4. Which aspect of predestination gives you the greatest comfort: past, present or future?

12

Guarding the good deposit

1:13–14

So what is Timothy to do, as he sits in his room, reading this letter? How is he to begin to put it into action? Paul begins to flesh out what is expected of Timothy, in two commands: there is a *pattern* which he must *keep*, and there is a *good deposit* which he must *guard*. In the first task he is promised the help of *Christ Jesus*, and in the second *the help of the Holy Spirit.*

KEEP THE PATTERN

Timothy must focus his energy on the *teaching* which Paul handed on to him. That teaching has two features here. The first is that it is *sound teaching*, and sound means healthy, or life-giving. So the teaching which Paul passed on to Timothy is good for us. The nearest explanation of that teaching is in verses 9–11.

Secondly, there is a distinctive *pattern* or shape to this teaching, which Timothy must have learned as he heard it. Again, what Paul has been arguing for in the preceding verses is critical, because the *pattern* Timothy must keep was that the authentic gospel will inevitably cause difficulties for those who proclaim it. This is the *pattern* that was being challenged in Timothy's day, and which he must cling to at all costs. When that gospel becomes increasingly difficult to believe as everyone around him abandons it, Timothy is to hold it with *faith* in Christ Jesus, whose life and ministry were marked by the same pattern. And when he is given harsh treatment because of his holding on, he is to treat his assailants with the same *love* that Christ Jesus showed his enemies as they crucified him. The lesson Paul wants Timothy to learn is continually pressed home: Jesus' ministry was shaped by the cross, that is now true of Paul, and he wants it to be true of Timothy.

GUARD THE TREASURE

The treasure, or *good deposit,* is the gospel itself, and the way of guarding it is to make sure it is taught clearly and well. To *guard* something is to protect it, and Paul is aware of the trends in the culture and churches that would be luring Timothy into allowing subtly different versions of the gospel into his ministry. So Timothy is to take responsibility for this precious treasure, and ensure that it is not lost or damaged during his watch.

So how did Paul *guard* the gospel, and how does he expect Timothy to do the same? Curiously, at first sight, by putting it on public view, where it can be knocked about by anyone who is passing. That is, Paul expects Timothy to engage in a public ministry of training teachers (2:2) and teaching the church (3:16). The gospel is not guarded by locking it up in a private vault. Rather, if it is being attacked it must be defended publicly, and if it is disbelieved he must win new converts (4:2–5). Timothy must guard it by taking action to protect it from error or half-truth. The rest of the letter will show how that will be done.

But once again Paul takes Timothy back to the key concern about whether Timothy has the resources for the task in hand, and reminds him that he will only be able to do this guarding *with the help of the Holy Spirit who lives in us,* the Holy Spirit who gave Timothy the *power ... love and ... self discipline* (1:7) to be a pastor.

Those twin tasks of keeping the pattern and guarding the treasure remain ours, especially if we are church leaders. The duty of passing on that pattern remains ours, as does the promise of the Holy Spirit, who lives not just in the apostle but *lives in us.* That must mean that the risks of failure are ours too. If Timothy, trained so well and over such a long period by Paul, was at risk of deviating, what hope do we have? If this man, of whom Paul said he *has proved himself, because as a son with a father he has served with me in the work of the gospel* (Philippians 2:22), was in tears over the demands of ministry and needed to be reminded of what he was to do, and that it was only possible with the presence of Jesus Christ and the power of the Holy Spirit, then could it be that our churches are as weak as they are because we have let our guard slip while we have been on duty? Have we allowed other, different messages to enter the minds and hearts of our church members?

Could it be that the reason we think Timothy was shy and unsuited to the task of ministry is that we have reinterpreted the task to be something other than what it was supposed to be – something that ought to be easily achieved by anyone halfway competent? Do we think that organising large meetings and running teams of assistants is so easy we would not employ a man with Timothy's weaknesses to do it? And all the while the task of passing on the pattern of a suffering gospel in a suffering ministry goes undone, and we hardly notice.

A task that reduced a giant like Timothy to tears, and which was only possible by the presence of Christ and the power of his Holy Spirit, is one we think can be achieved with relative ease and proven methodology. Perhaps we do not know enough to weep.

STUDY, DISCUSSION AND PRAYER

1. What can you do to ensure that the pattern of Paul's teaching is kept among the young Christians at your church?

2. If your church invited Timothy to be your pastor, what are the aspects you would expect him to guard? Since he is not coming, what are you going to do instead?

13

Desertion and friendship

1:15–18

Paul's perspective now widens to the church scene throughout the province of Asia, and to specific individuals who have helped or hindered him. The bare information may not have been news to Timothy, because Paul says *you know* about the hindrances, and *you know* about the character of the man who travelled from Ephesus to Rome to find him. But Paul is drawing lessons from these parallel examples, holding up each to Timothy in turn, and implicitly asking him which one he will be like. The lessons become explicit in 2:1.

DESERTION

We know nothing more of Phygelus and Hermogenes than what Paul says here, which is that they were known to him and to Timothy. Presumably they were known as strong Christians, and yet in a time of crisis they have *deserted* Paul. That must have come as an unpleasant shock, reminding Paul of the fragility of the bonds that tied him to the churches. After all, if high profile Christians such as these two find it hard to remain stable, then there is little hope for anyone else.

The wider scene bears that out, because Phygelus and Hermogenes are merely the named members of the far more worrying problem that *everyone in the province of Asia has deserted me.* This is an odd thing to say because it is superficially untrue: Timothy has not deserted Paul, nor has Onesiphorus in the next paragraph; Priscilla and Aquila have remained loyal, with some others (4:19). There is no indication that everyone in Asia has deserted the gospel or the church. But Paul has a narrow meaning in mind, and he is not exaggerating. Paul has a particular problem, which is that he is on trial, and he needs support in the manner of credible character witnesses. He is facing a series of charges of causing a public disturbance, a problem which had begun in Ephesus (Acts 19) and climaxed in Jerusalem (Acts 21). Trouble was gathering momentum behind him.

Part of Paul's defence was to give an accurate account of what had happened in Jerusalem, and the involvement in the day's events of an Ephesian Christian called Trophimus (Acts 21:29), and so he badly needed support – but it has melted into mist. To stand beside Paul and speak up for his good name, when he was already widely known as undesirable and shameful, was to be implicated in his disgrace, and for the Christians in Ephesus that had proved too high a price to pay. Those Christians who could have helped him were not now willing to swear in court to Paul's good intentions. Sadly that included even Christians of some reputation who slipped away quietly.

FRIENDSHIP

By contrast there is Onesiphorus, who is from *Ephesus* himself (although presumably not a witness to the riot), and he has made a deliberate and costly attempt to locate Paul and stay with him; *he often refreshed me.* In case we underestimate the difficulty Onesiphorus faced, it is worth considering the life Paul was living at the time. He was no longer under generous house arrest as at the end of Acts. He is in any one of the prisons in Rome.

The prisons in Rome were squalid and physically dangerous, and delays in court procedures meant that they were usually overcrowded way beyond their capacity. Unheated, sleep was almost impossible on the rough pallets or floor, with no bedding provided. Paul would also have been wearing heavy iron *chains*, perhaps linked to other prisoners to prevent anyone escaping. The iron, reacting to the prisoners' sweat, rusted, making their flesh rot; the heaviness weakened limbs already short of food, and (as many prisoners commented) the constant noise of chains on stone was yet another factor making sleep impossible. Food, beyond a meagre prison ration which was barely enough to sustain life, was the prisoner's own responsibility – but how could Paul, alone and cut off in Rome, arrange that? Lack of access to water meant that prisoners were not just filthy but frequently unrecognisable from the caked-on dirt and the matted beard and hair – for who would trust violent prisoners with access to a barber and his razors? Clothes rapidly reduce to rags in such circumstances. It is no wonder that prisons were associated not only with execution, but also with death from disease and, not infrequently, suicide.

One further obstacle lay in Onesiphorus' path as he traipsed the back streets of Rome trying to locate the prison which held Paul, and identify him among many thousands of prisoners. The prisons were airless and unhygienic because they were largely windowless. Obviously that prevented prisoners from getting out, but it also prevented much light from getting in. The more secure a cell was, the less light it would have had, and an underground cell would have had none at all. Onesiphorus was searching for an unrecognisable Paul among thousands of identical wretches, often in the pitch dark. No wonder Paul comments that *when he was in Rome, he searched hard for me until he found me.* Onesiphorus had performed a heroic labour of love.

What could have motivated him to undertake that time-consuming, unpleasant and frequently dangerous task? What could have driven him to persevere in the face of the stubbornness of petty officials and the nauseating visits to cell after cell? As each night he reflected on his failure to find Paul, and prepared to face another day's battle with red tape and hard heartedness, what stopped him packing up and going back to the household which was having to cope without him? Simply this, that he *was not ashamed of my chains.* He, unlike all the others in Asia, did not find it too much to be known as Paul's acquaintance.

In view of Paul's teaching on present suffering and future glory, it is not surprising that his way of rewarding Onesiphorus is to pray for him to *find mercy from the Lord on that day.* Once again, Paul's passion for the final coming of God's kingdom breaks through, because he knows that he has no other way of repaying his friend or of helping him in return. But Judgment Day will vindicate Paul, and all those who have allied with him in the cause of the gospel.

The charge to Timothy is gradually becoming clearer. Paul is suffering for the gospel, but he is *not ashamed* (1:12); Onesiphorus was unusual in being willing to be identified with this marked man, because he was *not ashamed*; and Timothy has already been put on notice that Paul thinks this is an issue for him: *do not be ashamed to testify about our Lord, or ashamed of me his prisoner. But join with me in suffering for the gospel* (1:8).

In the eyes of society as a whole, and in the eyes of the majority of Christians who had uncritically absorbed their society's values, Paul was a reject precisely because of his suffering. It will be a mark of how willing Timothy is to distance himself from those values and embrace the promises of the gospel instead, that he sees Paul's disgrace, and his Lord's disgrace, not as evidence of rejection by God but as the true pattern for Christians. To embrace Paul means to share his squalor and to face the same rejection from the world, and a worldly church.

STUDY, DISCUSSION AND PRAYER

1. What do you find most worrying about the story of Phygelus and Hermogenes? How can you guard against their mistakes?

2. What do you find most admirable about Onesiphorus? How can you build such behaviour into your relationships? Not having a personal relationship with Paul, how can you build such loyalty into your obedience toward his writings?

3. Now that the setting has become clearer about what is meant by being ashamed, are you becoming clearer about areas where you are tempted to be ashamed of Jesus, Paul or the gospel?

4. Pray about those areas.

14

Ability and reliability

2:1–2

It is usually the little connecting words such as 'and', 'but', or 'therefore' which show the flow of the argument in a document like this letter, and which help readers to keep the thread. In the first verse of Chapter 2 there is the small word 'then', which staples the beginning of Chapter 2 to the end of Chapter 1, and applies its lessons.

At the end of Chapter 1 Paul described Onesiphorus (1:16–17), and sketched out his costly loyalty. The key word for him was that he was *not ashamed*, and behind him were the sad lessons of 1:15, those who had deserted Paul – not because of the attraction of false teaching, but because of cowardice. That also lay behind Paul's concern for Timothy (1:7–8).

Paul draws all those lessons down on to Timothy. Don't be like Phygelus, Hermogenes and the others; instead, Timothy, be like Onesiphorus and *be strong*. That is, draw on the resources which the Holy Spirit gives, to enable us to suffer and stand.

My son is not only a note of affection, but puts Paul and Timothy in the kind of relationship described in the Book of Proverbs, where the tone is affection and spiritual teaching (Proverbs 1:8–10, and throughout the book). The connection between the two contains not only closeness but one learning from the other, and there are several ways this plays out in 2 Timothy: Apostle writing to Christian, experienced Christian leader to less-experienced leader, father to son, Teacher or Rabbi to pupil, example to follower and Master to apprentice.

But Paul has larger issues on his mind than Timothy's personal courage. Beyond Timothy he sees the church that he was pastoring. There were two pressures which that church faced. From inside, false teachers were challenging Paul's message with a triumphalist one of their own (2:18); and from the outside there was the continual presence of the state that was making all disciples pay a high price for loyalty to Christ (1:16), and in all likelihood these were linked. A Christian who was loyal to Paul would be persecuted by the culture and opposed by the false teachers. Equally, a Christian who was loyal to the false teachers would be ignored or even applauded by the culture but would desert Paul and the true gospel. Timothy's mentor and his church's membership stand in opposite corners pulling him in opposite directions.

The pressures this pastor faced are not new, nor are they unique. When one part of the membership of a church begins to be drawn into error the temptation among those who remain, particularly for the leaders, is to draw the circle ever tighter, becoming a clique or club which defines itself over against the world and has nothing to do with it, never engaging with it or saving people from it. Paul, however, has a different plan for Timothy and his church. Timothy must think strategically and recruit staff for growth and action, and he needs people to stand by him with two qualifications. The particular Greek word translated *men* here is one which does not indicate gender, and at this point Paul is not making a point about male/female relationships within the local church. Because the term *men* is so loaded today, it probably helpful to translate the word with the more neutral – and more accurate – *people.*

- **They must be people of reliability.** Unlike Phygelus and Hermogenes, but like Onesiphorus, the next generation of Christian leaders must have backbone.

- **They must be people of ability.** In a church tempted by false teachers, Timothy's appointees must have the brains in order to be able to teach truth well.

These two qualifications are both essential and work together. People who have brains without backbone permit the Church to drift, because they will never stand for their own convictions and will prefer to avoid conflict. They will be able to see both sides of every question but will never be able to decide which is right. On the other hand, people who have backbone without brains will permit the Church to become irrelevant because they will always fight yesterday's battles again, never having the flexibility to think afresh about new questions. So Timothy is to look for leaders who will have both brains and backbone, to appoint people of ability and reliability.

This process, usually called 'discipling', is one that has rightly found a home in many organisations and student bodies, but is alien to many contemporary churches. This is odd, because it is clearly one that goes back to Jesus himself, in common with other Rabbis of his day. Jesus worked with the idea of concentric 'circles of influence', distinguishing the crowd from his disciples, because *he did not say anything to (the public) without using a parable. But when he was alone with his own disciples, he explained everything* (Mark 4:34). Later he distinguished the seventy-two (Luke 10:1), the Twelve (Luke 6:12–16), and within them the Three (Peter, James and John [Luke 9:28]). Jesus gave increasingly intensive training to those who were intended to be future teachers and leaders.

Timothy had seen, and been part of, the same process in Paul's ministry. Churches were started and supported with a lifeline of teaching, letters and visits. But in Acts 16 – 20 the likes of Timothy are exposed to models of church planting and nurturing, teaching and ministry that would have implanted necessary lessons for the years ahead. Now Timothy is to put that model into action.

What Timothy is to pass on to these people, and what they in their turn will be required to transmit to a further generation, is what Timothy *heard me say in the presence of many witnesses.* Yet again Timothy is involved in a chain of loyalty. He is himself to keep the pattern he heard from Paul (1:13), Paul himself was appointed to his ministry by God and the Lord Jesus associates himself with the suffering Paul (1:8; 11–12a). So the pattern which Timothy is to pass on is not only the faithful gospel outline, but the necessary implication that believing the gospel will involve the Christian in costly discipleship (3:12, Acts 9:15–16).

So this verse is a call to loyalty. God has communicated the genuine message to Paul (1:11), Paul has communicated it to Timothy (1:13), and now Timothy has to communicate it to others, and the others to yet another group. Presumably if that group is taught properly it will in its turn pass the message on yet further. It is a breathtakingly large vision from a man in a prison cell.

In the context of a church facing false teaching, the correct course of action is to train and deploy good teachers. So whether one is a church leader, someone in training for full time Christian work, or a mature Christian with some responsibility for others in a church, if our churches are going to be loyal to Christ in the twenty-first century we must grasp from the outset that there will be false teachers to buffet us, whom we must resist, and cultural crosscurrents to cause us to drift, which we must also resist. We need to plan and prepare for the existence of loyal Christian teachers in our churches. The way to resist is not running away to a safe distance but to engage in spiritual warfare.

Planning, on the basis of 2:2, means we shall need to learn how to disciple a small group of future leaders, to spend time with them and expose them to the principles of church leadership. The principles which Timothy saw at first hand are clearly visible in both Acts and Paul's letters, and the model for it is the pattern of Jesus' training for the future.

It is all too easy to assume that that 'discipling' is something that takes place for the first few weeks or months of a new Christian's life, to get him or her over the initial hurdles of believing. We can think that teaching is something that happens only on Sundays, from the front, in a pulpit, and that training is best done in a theological college from behind a lecturer's lectern. But Timothy's challenge is to provide long term, intensive, closely watched and intimate training for a few, in order to provide adequately for the needs of the church for the future.

STUDY, DISCUSSION AND PRAYER

1. Which is your tendency: brains without backbone or backbone without brains?

2. What is the training for future leaders in your church? How could it be improved? Or, if there is none, how could it be started and what should it cover?

3. Identify two or three people you could influence to become increasingly faithful. How could you do that?

4. Who have been the greatest influences on your Christian growth?

5. Give thanks for those who have been the greatest influences on your Christian growth. Pray for them that they will continue to impact on other Christians.

15

The coward, the cheat and the slacker

2:3–7

War is hard – it costs lives, and is awful and painful. But it is an appropriate way of understanding the clash between God and sin, and the way in which Christian leaders are *soldiers.* 'Is Timothy a *good soldier*?' asks Paul.

Imagine that one day a man decides to join the army. He finds the nearest barracks and walks into the office of the captain. He says that he would like to enlist because he has always rather fancied the uniform. Khaki is his colour. He likes the idea of travelling the world, he enjoys marching and bands, the pomp appeals to him, ever since he was young he has dreamt of driving a tank, and he once had an enjoyable holiday camping. He thinks that being in the army would be fun, and he would like to sign up that day.

He would, of course, be a fool. Within three months he might find himself with a UN peacekeeping force facing real bullets, real bombs, and real land-mines. He signed up hoping for a smart uniform. He suddenly realises he faces the prospect of wearing a body bag.

So when Paul tells Timothy to endure hardship with him like a good soldier, he is drawing a tough and possibly shocking comparison for a Christian leader. Timothy was discovering that being a pastor is not easy. There were days, even weeks, when he wondered why he bothered to enlist. It was not turning out to be the job that he thought he was going to do. So in verses 4–6 Paul strengthens him with three famous pictures of Christian leadership facing hardship – the soldier, the athlete, and the farmer.

It is important that these are seen in the context of the letter as a whole. For example, the picture of the soldier on its own might lead to strange ideas about what a civilian pursuit might be. Could it be the distraction of being married? Might it mean that a Christian minister must be full-time, without other employment? The word athlete on its own could suggest that there are rules for Christian ministers which must be kept – prayer, Bible study, Church leadership etc. These things not wrong, of course, but they are not to the forefront of Paul's thinking. Likewise the share of the crops enjoyed by the farmer might make a church think it is being told to reimburse their pastor properly.

However, when we place these illustrations side by side, and place them into 2 Timothy, other points emerge.

The most obvious theme is one of potential failure. These three illustrations have a negative feel to them. Civilian affairs are not neutral for a soldier – and certainly not when there is a war on. It would be ludicrous for a soldier to take time out from a battle in order to run a shop or mow a lawn. That is not what he is employed to do. Rather he is to stand his ground. When there is a war on the soldier's place is in the front line, facing the bullets. Desertion is our contemporary word for the temptation to return to civilian affairs. It leads to a court martial, and once led to being shot.

The athlete continues the theme of failure. What happens to an athlete who doesn't compete according to the rules? What does popular opinion think of an athlete who tops up on steroids, the racing driver who drives an illegally designed car, or a jockey who lies about his weight? They are cheats. It is not a nice word – it is sordid, and filled with shame.

Similarly the farmer faces hard work, in all weathers, all seasons, and all personal circumstances. Whatever he feels like, weeds still grow and plants still need watering. Why does he need to turn out all the time? Because the alternative is no food, no money, no house.

It could almost be said that these three pictures are not of a soldier, an athlete, or a farmer at all. Rather, they are pictures of a cowardly soldier, a cheating athlete, and a warning to a slack farmer.

Another theme that links at least two of these pictures is of the future. Olympic officials do not dash on to the track, slinging a winner's medal around the neck of the athlete who currently happens to be leading the pack. They wait by the finishing line to see who crosses it first. Similarly the farmer cannot enjoy the crops until the harvest is in and finished. For Paul, of course, prize day and harvest day are deferred until the future – resurrection day (4:8). Timothy is ministering in the thick of the battle, the middle of a marathon, and the hard part of the growing season. Medals and celebrations are yet to come.

Of course there are great promises in these pictures. Timothy is told he can please the Lord Jesus Christ – that is a great promise. As is receiving a victor's crown. But there is an indication that Paul is concerned that Timothy might give up – or, at least, that the people he appoints might give up.

These three pictures can be taken further. Timothy is to recruit, teach and train people of ability and reliability to a ministry of teaching and therefore of suffering. What would these three pictures mean for them? How could a Christian leader run away from the front line? The answer lies in everything seen so far in the desertions of 1:15, and Paul's fears for Timothy in 1:8. It lies in Timothy's potential failure to stay in the front line of fire over the false teachers, and showing signs of wavering in the face of his culture. If we think we would have done better, imagine what courage it would have taken to lead a series of Bible studies on the resurrection in the church Timothy pastored. It is painfully obvious what form cowardice takes for a Christian minister, and we know that it doesn't please Christ.

How could a Christian leader cheat or cut corners in ministry? By not delivering the whole message and cutting out the hard parts. In 1:8 Paul reminded Timothy of the inevitability of suffering as a Christian, but that has never been an attractive or popular message. To cheat would be to pass on the gospel without the suffering, the gospel without its edges, a bland and easy gospel. In recruiting potential leaders it is too easy to play down the hardship, but that means that the next generation does not get the accurate message. So they will not have the spiritual equipment to stand firm themselves. Was Timothy cutting corners to make life easy for himself?

Being a farmer is a life of sheer, hard slog. So, says Paul, training new leaders is not a one-off event but a long-term process. Engaging in hardship is not a one-off difficulty but a long-term challenge.

This is a lesson every Christian leader needs to learn. It is one that Paul wants us to learn, and one that God himself wants to teach us. When facing difficulty in our churches and the world, battered by a constant sense of failure and the apparent successful churches which promote cheap Christianity, we might, with Timothy, be tempted to quit. But Paul tells us to mine these three pictures deeply, and the God who calls us to Christian ministry, and who stands with us as we minister, will teach us and help us to learn.

STUDY, DISCUSSION AND PRAYER

1. What might tempt you to be a coward? What are the civilian pursuits which might persuade you not to fight? How could you be encouraged to be more brave?

2. How might you be tempted to cheat or cut corners? How might you be encouraged to keep the rules?

3. Where are you tempted to be idle? What might encourage you to be more hardworking?

4. As you think over what Paul wrote, have other lessons have come to mind?

16

Bondage and freedom

2:8–10

CHAINS

Once again, Paul carefully links the gospel he longs to communicate with the price he is paying for it in his prisoner's *chains.* The careful reader has understood that by now, and so, presumably, has Timothy. So it is rather surprising for him to be told to *remember* it. How could he forget?

The answer is, that in the close work of Christian ministry, it is actually shockingly easy. The big picture, and the logic of the gospel, can be lost in the pressures of life.

Timothy must make an effort to focus on the most important points, particularly when they are being distorted by others. He is to *remember Jesus Christ.* This is the only time *Jesus Christ* is called that in this letter. Elsewhere he is always referred to as *Christ Jesus.* Perhaps the reversal of names here is to put a subtle emphasis on the humanity of Jesus, to remind Timothy that his suffering came before his glory.

Timothy is to remember that he was *raised from the dead, descended from David,* and again it is possible to see that as a subtle reversal. Jesus was born before he was raised from the dead but Paul puts it the other way around. Remember Jesus' resurrection, he says, and remember his royalty, but do not let the glory obscure what happened before.

From the first Christian sermon (Acts 2) the right of Jesus to be called *Son of David* was being teased out. It was obviously a royal title, but Jesus had already raised the puzzling fact that Psalm 110 states that the Messiah was going to be even greater than his illustrious ancestor; so much greater, in fact, that David was going to acknowledge him as his Lord (Luke 20:41–44).

As David's Psalms were read further it became clear that he expected this great descendant to be an eternal king who would defy death and be the rightful inheritor of all the promises made to David and his royal line (Acts 2:25–36). God had promised David that *When your days are over and you go to be with your fathers, I will raise up your offspring to succeed you, one of your own sons, and I will establish his kingdom. He is the one who will build a house for me, and I will establish his throne forever. I will be his father, and he will be my son. I will never take my love away from him, as I took it away from your predecessor. I will set him over my house and my kingdom forever; his throne will be established forever* (1 Chronicles 17:11–14). God's promise to David was that there would be a future king who would be both *one of your own sons* and *my son.* That double promise became the foundation for all the various subsequent promises about the coming Messiah, and it became common to talk of the king, David's Son, as God's Son (Psalm 2:7). The phrase *Son of God* was a royal title, and to be the inheritor of it was to be the inheritor of all the others that depend upon it.

The obvious candidate was King Solomon, David's direct successor, but he failed morally, and he also failed by dying. A dead king is not able to have a *throne forever.* So the waiting for a future king began. When Jesus was *raised from the dead* it was as a consequence of his being the promised one who was *descended from David,* and it is one of the highest honours that could be his. It means he is thc Son of David, and the Son of God, who will reign forever.

The link between the gospel and Paul's prisoner status is that it is precisely this gospel (and no other) which has landed Paul in chains, *the gospel (God) promised beforehand through his prophets in the Holy Scriptures regarding his Son, who as to his human nature was a descendant of David, and who through the Spirit of holiness was declared with power to be the Son of God, by his resurrection from the dead: Jesus Christ our Lord* (Romans 1:2–4). Jesus had always been and always will be God's Son in the sense that the creeds talk about. He always existed as the second person of the Trinity, but Resurrection Day was the day when God the Son became the royal *Son of God,* and all the Old Testament prophecies about his suffering and his glory were fulfilled.

Contemporary success-driven Christianity needs to learn this lesson as much as Timothy: in God's great plan the message of a glorious king who suffered is best carried by a messenger who is chained like a criminal but is hoping for God's kingdom (1:1). If losing the chains means losing the gospel, and keeping the gospel means keeping the chains, would contemporary Christians make the right choice?

FREEDOM

Roman emperors do not like to hear of rival kings, with an ancient lineage and an eternal throne. But although they can chain the messenger they cannot chain the message, and Paul knows that beyond his walls more and more people believe it. Indeed, the very fact of his inability to spread it and yet its growing success shows that God, not Paul, is its master and it is uncontainable by prison bars. God's word is not chained. And if it spreads not despite but because of Paul being in chains, then it is the genuine gospel because the genuine gospel is not afraid of suffering. Paul's weakness is the perfect backdrop to show off the gospel's glory.

ENDURANCE

Such is Paul's identification with Jesus and the cross, that he sees that his ministry has a similar pattern to his master's. He suffers on behalf of others. The pattern is the familiar one from the earlier part of the letter: it is *the salvation that is in Christ Jesus, with eternal glory.* That is, Paul cannot mention salvation without drawing attention to its future, glorious aspect, because only a glorious future would make sense of his grimy present. The experience of Christian ministry matches the time scale of the Christian message (grime and glimpses of glory now, and full glory later), and the elect who are won by Jesus' death (1:9–10) are reached by Christians who adopt that pattern for their lives. Paul's apostolic ministry is unique, but he is still giving instructions to Timothy about what is to be taught to faithful teachers (2:2). Next he is going to make certain that the lesson is learnt by everyone (2:11–22).

STUDY, DISCUSSION AND PRAYER

1. What aspects of Jesus' life and ministry are you most tempted to forget?

2. How can you make sure that you remember Jesus' humanity, suffering and death?

3. How can you make sure you remember Jesus' glory and eternal reign?

4. Pray for Christians in a country where you know it is hard to be a believer. Pray that *they* will trust that God's word is not chained.

17

If we, then he

2:11–13

This slightly poetic section is one of the famous 'faithful sayings' of the Pastoral letters (1 Timothy 1:15; 3:1; 4:9, Titus 3:8) in which Paul seems to distil his teaching point into a particularly memorable phrase or form. They do not rhyme, but have a strong rhythm and pattern. Paul has written four points introduced by *if*, with each line having a balancing second half, except the last which has a double ending. Paul wants his readers to stop and consider carefully what he says. He is no longer talking about himself alone, but Timothy, his trainees, indeed, everyone who reads this letter.

DEATH

The first section is a simple promise of resurrection for every dead Christian. He puts *died* in a past tense presumably because he is imagining looking back over a completed life where the Christian's long fight for loyalty is over. In a church where even a doctrine as basic as resurrection was being questioned, this is an essential starting point. Those who have remained loyal to Christ in this life will remain with him in the next.

ENDURANCE

Jesus' faithfulness extends to rewarding those who suffer on his behalf. The focus has shifted subtly, because *endure* is in the present tense, probably meaning 'if we carry on enduring'. That is Paul's present, hard experience in prison, where he is willing to *endure everything for the sake of the elect* that they may share *eternal glory* (2:10). And now Paul is drawing Timothy into the same movement.

DISOWNING

Here is the terrible warning which stands over the head of many of the deserters in Ephesus and Rome, for these are the people who refuse to *endure*, and instead deny Jesus. Their attitude is probably more indicative of a direction in life than a momentary giving way to pressure, one weakness leading on to further weakness, and an action becoming a cast of mind. It is far better to steel oneself in advance by mulling over this powerful warning.

FAITHFUL

God can never be *faithless*, he will always stand by his word. This means that both his promises and warnings in these verses are true and unbreakable, and that God's eternal plan will not fail because of the failure of Christians. His church will stand.

So this last clause is double edged for Timothy. He can rely on God to *remain faithful* if he continues to *endure*, and he should take it as a warning should he give up. Whether he remains faithful to the task or not, God will make sure it continues because he *cannot disown himself.*

STUDY, DISCUSSION AND PRAYER

1. Which of the four sections in these verses do you most need to remember, and why?

2. Is God's plan for the future a factor in your everyday thinking and living? How might thinking about God's plan for the future affect your relationships and activities at work, home and with your friends?

3. Do you think that Timothy heard the final section as an encouragement or a warning? How do you hear it?

4. Pray that God's Spirit would enable you to endure and not deny Christ. Give thanks that he remains faithful in spite of our faithlessness.

18

An unashamed worker

2:14–18

Timothy's task is to draw down those important lessons into the practical reality of everyday church life, and to keep *reminding them* (presumably meaning the trainee teachers of 2:2, but it would have been a lesson the whole church needed to hear) *of these things* concerning lifelong loyalty. Timothy is to impress upon his apprentices precisely the same lessons that Paul is pressing upon him. At this stage it is about how to keep on with the task of teaching in a quarrelsome, chattering, and potentially deviant church.

WORDS

The first lesson they have to learn is the danger of being side-tracked into fruitless discussion. The problem is *quarrelling about words,* three words in English to translate one word in the original, which means something like 'splitting hairs'. Paul is no enemy to clarity of thought or expression, and he frequently engaged in close debate and argument, but he is warning Timothy there is an attitude of mind which engages in speculative and divisive word-games, and that is to be avoided. The clearest example arises in verse 17 (see below), but it is enough here to see it as a general warning about abusing the role of the teacher by showing oneself to be clever, or of having a deeper and more subtle understanding of the Bible than a plain reading of the text would give.

There is *no value* in such teaching, and the *only* result of their hours of puzzles is that it *ruins those who listen*; but put such people in a church where there is a teacher who is trying to teach simply and clearly, and the result is *quarrelling about words.* On one side would have been Timothy, steeped in the scriptures since his youth, and on the other someone who had constructed a distorted version of the gospel by getting various elements out of proportion, and importing or omitting important ideas. But to *those who listen,* a debate between those two is utterly ruinous. How is a new Christian to decide who is right? The result is confusion on the part of the teachers and ineffectiveness on the part of Timothy. His young trainees must learn to avoid the time-wasters.

This lesson is a serious one, and Timothy must *warn them before God* about it. It would be a terrible blunder for them to think that they were doing the right thing by spending time on this issue, if the end result is that the main membership of the church is left unable to trust its own teachers or to distinguish truth from error. Serious debate and dialogue is one thing, but wasting time with people who make a hobby of obscure interpretation is quite another.

WORK

It will be far more fruitful if they avoid obscurity altogether and stick to the main road of Bible teaching. To be told that one's teaching is *of no value, and only ruins those who listen* would be devastating; how much better to have that ministry *approved* by God.

What Timothy and his apprentices need to do first is to remember that they are exercising a teaching ministry on God's behalf and they are accountable to him for what they say. So the teaching ministry is to be conducted with a clear expectation of God's ongoing scrutiny and final judgment. Teachers are to remember that the most important person in the congregation is God himself, and it is his approval or disapproval which counts.

A preacher who speaks to many hundreds has a great motivation to do the hard work of understanding the Bible before preaching, otherwise he will look a fool and perhaps be rebuked by his fellow-leaders. But Paul wants these people to stick to their task when they are leading a Bible study group of four, when there are only twenty in church, and when the wider Christian church seems to be following a lie.

They need to be *workmen*, putting in the time to work at a passage or book, until they have it crystal clear, and making the message so straightforward that the people they teach wonder why they spend hours doing it because it is so obvious. Paul has deliberately used a hard, physical word for what looks like a soft, intellectual activity, to remind us that faithfulness to the whole of God's word takes time – years, in fact, of constant effort.

The good teacher will remain a student, always dissatisfied with the present level of understanding, determined that he *correctly handles the word of truth. Correctly handles* translates an engineer's term for making sure that the road cut through a hill was as straight as a Roman road should be, without deviation, and marking out the clearest path for those who follow. Because other people in Timothy's church are busy building a by-pass.

WANDERING

There are some people who have a different teaching; or, to translate more literally to make the point more clearly, they have a rival 'word' to the *word of truth* with which Timothy spends his time. This is clearly not the earlier group of verse 14: these are no argumentative amateurs, but some highly placed and well-known individuals. Little is known about *Hymenaeus and Philetus*, but what there is, is devastating. These men were once orthodox Christians, believing what Paul and Timothy believed. They must have been, because the only way to *wander away from the truth* is to have believed it in the first place and then to have moved. Their movement has been over time, and Paul and Timothy have tried to arrest it before because Hymenaeus was the object of Paul's discipline in 1 Timothy 1:20. Whatever Paul did then, and whatever it was for, it did not stop a determined troublemaker recruiting another co-leader and now numerous followers.

What is more, they still masquerade as Christians, because they are using Christian language. The *resurrection* is the doctrine they have distorted here. The first lesson to learn is that just because high profile teachers used to be Bible-believing Christians is no guarantee that they are still Bible-believing Christians; and the second lesson is that just because they have stopped being Bible-believing Christians does not stop them using biblical vocabulary. A great many churches and denominations have officials today who once would have stood where Timothy stood, but have now moved; and although they will say they have 'evangelical roots', what that means is that they no longer call themselves evangelicals. They have *wandered away from the truth.*

Hymenaeus and Philetus are typical at this point, in the way they handle the crucial doctrine of the resurrection. *They say that the resurrection has already taken place.* The details of that are needed for understanding the rest of 2 Timothy, but it is important to notice on the way that their method is to use an orthodox word but reinterpret its meaning. They want still to be called Christians, and to do that they have to have a doctrine of the resurrection, but they do not want the orthodox one. Like taxidermists stuffing the skin of an animal with straw, they have removed the vital parts of 'resurrection' and stuffed the word with heresy. But they still use the word.

By *the resurrection,* of course, they mean that the chain of events which began with Jesus' resurrection had run its full course in their present experience. The Old Testament had begun to look forward to a day when everyone would be raised from the dead, either to salvation or judgment (Daniel 12:2). Christians said that that had been confirmed and initiated by the resurrection of Jesus and his subsequent enthronement in heaven as saviour and judge (Acts 2:25–36). Christians, said Paul, have been raised with Christ and are seated with Christ (Ephesians 2:6), and that determines his entire understanding of who we are and how we should live. But that was not the end – far from it. Christians look forward to the great Resurrection day, when our sin and mortality will be done away with for ever and Jesus *will transform our lowly bodies so that they will be like his glorious body* (Philippians 3:21).

Hymenaeus and Philetus have collapsed all that future hope into the here and now. The precise contours of their error are lost, which is just as well because no one today would believe exactly what they taught. But the root of the problem that Paul describes is still common. Take, at one extreme, the hyper-enthusiasm of those who believe that all the future promises are realised in their present experience. It is physically impossible for them to be sick; indeed, sickness is a sign of lack of belief because a believing Christian should be able to claim all the blessings.

A Christian who sins is sub-Christian, because sin belongs to the old nature, and now we have a new nature. Paul's subtle work of understanding how it is that sin can be both abnormal and yet a present experience (Romans 7 – 8) has been lost in a torrent of fulfilled prophecy. Heaven is present on earth, and Jesus is present among his people in such a tangible way, that there is almost no need for the resurrection to occur. It has already happened. The result, which history shows takes a while to work out but comes inevitably, is first doubt and then cynicism. People who have been burned by hyper-enthusiasm will think all living churches are similarly manipulating and self-deluding. And they stop believing. Or, as Paul puts it, their churches *say that the resurrection has already taken place, and they destroy the faith of some* (2:18).

Then, at a different extreme, there are the worldly-wise church leaders who have lost belief in the supernatural reality of Christianity. For them, Christian doctrine is a social construct, a way of interpreting reality, along with many other such constructs. If Christianity is merely a matter of words, it cannot be taken in any way literally; indeed, to take it literally is crude and unsophisticated. Words such as 'miracle', 'resurrection' and even 'God' are metaphors, ways of re-describing reality to disclose a deeper level of meaning. To ask a naive question about whether Jesus' tomb was empty, or whether our own graves will be, is to misunderstand what language does. Talking about 'resurrection', whether Jesus' or our own, is a powerful image for talking about hope, but no more than a powerful image. There is no great Resurrection Day to look forward to, but if we have 'hope' we have everything that the metaphor is intended to provoke. Resurrection has already happened.

By now, a reader has either understood the point and seen the danger of this position, or switched off. In either case, Paul was right. People who sit under such teaching will find that their faith has been destroyed. The teachers will say it has been 're-described' but Paul knows better. For a first-century orthodox Christian, resurrection meant physical, bodily resurrection. It meant more than that, of course, because it involved transformation into the glorious likeness to Christ, but it certainly meant no less. The person who leads a church and holds to deviant teaching will destroy the faith of those who listen, either because they follow it or because they get so bewildered they walk out. *They say the resurrection has already taken place, and they destroy the faith of some.*

One common factor that such forms of Christianity share is that they present themselves as 'advanced' or 'progressive'. God is doing something new and different, and whether it is a spectacular new form of supernaturalism or a new reinterpretation of old truth, it is cutting edge. Surprisingly, Paul agrees. Indeed, he says they are progressive, but in two unhelpful ways.

First, those who engage in such teaching *will become more and more ungodly*. That is, an error will always lead to another, greater one, because an error is naturally off-centre and deviant. Someone who denies the hope of the resurrection in some way or other will inevitably deny other things which depend on it, like the uniqueness of Jesus or the need to repent of our sins. Christian truth is a united way of talking about God, where each part of his revelation is connected to the others, and if there is damage at one part it will damage all the other parts to which it is joined. Corruption at one point will inevitably spread. The word *ungodly* indicates the direction the horrible progress takes, because it means action or conduct. It is impossible for doctrinal error to remain doctrinal error; it will force itself out into moral error, out of the realm of belief into the realm of behaviour.

There are many churches and denominations around the world which sat loose to issues of doctrine in the 1960s and 1970s which are discovering that there is considerable pressure to change their attitudes on morality; that is no coincidence, for the two are intimately connected. If Paul is right, unless we tackle the underlying doctrinal problem there will be pressure to accept *more and more ungodly* behaviour, and we should expect to see things which currently appal us being debated within our boards and synods in the next fifteen to twenty years.

The second kind of progress that Paul warns Timothy about is that this teaching will be hugely successful in the short term, and potentially corrupt the entire Christian community where he works. *Their teaching,* he says, *will spread like gangrene.* Ironically, a teaching about the resurrection will have the stink of death about it, but it will spread. Not forever, and not terminally, as he goes on to say, but it will spread like rottenness in an open wound.

There is evidence of the spread all through 2 Timothy, with quite senior leaders becoming affected by it, whether like these two men, they have come to believe the error, and like Demas (4:10) merely been influenced by it, or like Timothy, surprised by its impact and rather nonplussed over how to proceed in the face of its plausibility to his members. If this teaching is going to *spread like gangrene* though his city and the church he leads, what can he do other than watch?

STUDY, DISCUSSION AND PRAYER

1. Does your Bible study ever become a pointless 'dispute about words'? How can you keep a better sense of proportion?

2. If you are a leader or teacher, how much time do you spend in preparation? Would you describe your approach as adequately workmanlike?

3. Can you identify the kind of groups who say *the resurrection has already happened today*? How might their influence be held back in your church?

4. Pray for anyone you know whose faith has been shaken by false teaching.

19

God's solid foundation

2:19

The solution for Timothy is to begin with what God has actually promised about his building-work in the world, his church. From Timothy's perspective it looks worryingly fragile and unstable, much as our own churches do today, perhaps, but *nevertheless*, despite the temporary battles, *God's foundation stands firm.* Paul is probably echoing an earlier promise from Isaiah, given at a time of national and spiritual collapse and imminent judgment. *See, I lay a stone in Zion, a tested stone, a precious cornerstone for a sure foundation; the one who trusts will never be dismayed* (Isaiah 28:16). In other words, says Paul, whether it is the invading armies of Babylon or the corrosive forces of error, nothing can remove God's eternal purposes.

The cornerstone is probably to be identified with 'the church' in its widest sense, meaning God's saved people, whom he has covenanted will be with him for eternity. Individual congregations might come and go, and the lack of a Christian church today in many of the places where Paul planted them is an example of that. But the fact that there are believers today, and believers who read this letter, proves Paul's point, that *God's solid foundation stands firm.*

God has placed his mark of ownership, his *seal,* on it twice.

THE SEAL OF OWNERSHIP

The first quotation comes from Numbers 16:5, where Moses was facing a major revolt against his leadership, led by Korah and over two hundred and fifty other respected leaders. Moses' response to the challenge is to allow God to decide who should lead Israel, him or the rebels, and God is able to do this because *the Lord will show who belongs to him* (Paul is paraphrasing slightly here, perhaps quoting the Greek Old Testament).

The point for Timothy is that the muddle and confusion he sees around him, with uncertainty over whom to trust and whom to discipline, is not mirrored in heaven. God is completely clear who is in his church and who is not, and Hymenaeus and Phyletus do not belong. Timothy may find it hard to remove them, their teaching and their influence from the congregation, but the Lord *knows who are his,* and will preserve them.

THE SEAL OF OBEDIENCE

The second seal God places on his church is that the people he owns will display a desire to obey him when they are told what is right and what is wrong. There are numerous scriptures Paul is alluding to here, and he is highlighting a general trend rather than a particular text, but two are perhaps more prominent than others. The first is Isaiah 26:13, *O Lord, our God, other lords besides you have ruled over us, but your name alone do we honour,* which highlights the importance of respecting God's reputation as sole Lord. The other possibility is Leviticus 24:16, *anyone who blasphemes the name of the Lord must be put to death.* Paul does not advocate the punishment because churches have a different legal standing before God to Israel's, but he does identify rebellion with blasphemy, which is appropriate in 2 Timothy.

The mark of true Christians in Ephesus will be that when error is pointed out, and they are shown that it leads to *wickedness,* they will turn back to truth and obedience. It may not be possible for Timothy to make this judgment on any congregation as a whole, but he can make it a demand on individuals.

STUDY, DISCUSSION AND PRAYER

1. Are there any issues in your church that make you fear it may not stand?

2. Are you tempted to guess who is 'in' God's kingdom by external appearances?

3. What are the areas where you know you have not been obeying God? What are the areas of wickedness in society that your church needs to turn away from?

4. Do you think there will always be Christians in our country?

5. Pray for Christians in government.

20

Useful to the master

2:20–26

LIFE IN THE LARGE HOUSE

A large house conjures images of gracious living and domestic staff, cut glass and silver in the dining room, and everyday plates downstairs. Paul's imagery here of a *large house* may be a domestic one, with *gold and silver* for the fortunate few and *wood and clay* for the cook and butler to use. That would be enough to make his point.

It is possible, though, that he is still dealing in Old Testament imagery, and that there is an allusion here which gives a deeper layer of meaning, although not substantially different in content. When King David planned to build the original temple, he told his son, Solomon, who would accomplish the task, that *I have taken great pains to provide for the temple of the LORD a hundred thousand talents of gold, a million talents of silver, quantities of bronze and iron too great to be weighed, and wood and stone. And you may add to them* (1 Chronicles 22:14). The reason was that *the house to be built for the LORD should be of great magnificence and fame and splendour in the sight of all the nations* (1 Chronicles 22:5).

If that passage lies at the back of Paul's mind here, as he transfers to the church the blessings associated with the temple, and compares that *house* to God's great, or *large house,* he is reminding Timothy that the church he pastors is where God has chosen to live. He must treat his task with the seriousness and reverence with which the users of the original temple treated theirs. In this place where God dwells there are two kinds of articles, different in their nature, being either precious metal or cheap disposable materials, and therefore differing in their purpose. They will be used for either serving at the place of sacrifices and assisting the priests, or cleaning up afterwards. Timothy is to handle them with discretion.

The difficulty is to work out how this applies to Timothy, because he is to cleanse himself from *the latter* (that is, the *ignoble purposes*) so that he can be the more valuable kind of instrument. Unlike the vessels in the temple, which are made of one kind of thing and cannot change their nature, it is possible for Timothy to *cleanse* himself of impurities and so become able to serve God more usefully.

There are two ways that this can be taken. One is to say that the two kinds of vessels in the house refer to two kinds of teachers in the church, true and false. If Timothy can remove the false teachers from their positions he will have cleansed the temple. This illustration would then refer back to 2:14–19, and the rivals he faces. The difficulty with this understanding is that it makes Timothy's task to cleanse the church, where Paul's point is that he must *cleanse himself*. There must be a better explanation, which is more internalised for Timothy.

The second way is to say that the two kinds of vessels refer to two kinds of teaching (rather than teachers), and that Timothy is to remove false doctrine from himself. For those who hold to a high view of Timothy that is almost unthinkable, but if a more worrying picture of Timothy is drawn where he is perhaps being influenced by the errors around him, then it is plausible. In this case the illustration would not refer backwards, but would flag a new area of concern, which is how Timothy is to think and act differently, not only from the people causing trouble, but even from his current practice.

There is the idea of false teaching (2:17) and true teaching (2:25) in the immediate context, and Paul now turns to how Timothy can *cleanse himself* of error and its far reaching tentacles. He lists fourteen characteristics that mark *the Lord's servant.*

THE LORD'S SERVANT IS MARKED BY ...

Purity

Hebrews reminds us that in the Temple, and its predecessor the Tabernacle, *the law requires that nearly everything be cleansed with blood* (Hebrews 9:22). Although Paul's point here is slightly different, because the blood motif is not in his mind, the requirement that Timothy *cleanses himself* finds it root in the same ritual. The vessels which were most holy were subject to constant cleaning. So Timothy is to keep himself and his teaching 'clean' from the pollution of the error around him. He is to keep a close watch on his doctrine.

Holiness

To be *made holy* is temple language again, because anything which God owns is his exclusive property. As the Lord told Moses when describing the gifts people promise to give him, *nothing that a man owns and devotes to the LORD – whether man or animal or family land – may be sold or redeemed; everything so devoted is most holy to the LORD* (Leviticus 27:28). To be *made holy* is to be God's personal possession and to share his moral perfection.

In one sense, Timothy, like all Christians, was already *holy*, because he was owned by God. We have all been *washed ... sanctified* (that is, made holy) and *justified in the name of the Lord Jesus Christ and by the Spirit of our God* (1 Corinthians 6:11). But Paul means a secondary truth here, which is that Timothy is to watch himself, particularly in the moral arena, where so much damage was being done by Paul's opponents (3:2–5).

Usefulness

Now that Timothy can recognise the error and its fruit, and is able to take on the task of being a model to younger Christians, he will be *useful to the Master.*

Preparedness

If Paul's teaching is effective then Timothy will be working to overcome his reluctance, and will be *prepared to do any good work,* whether it is to his taste or not, whether teaching the truth or combating error. He will once more be the front-line soldier, the disciplined athlete, and the hardworking farmer.

Maturity

Timothy is to *flee the evil desires of youth.* Again, the tighter the focus here the more relevant will be Paul's teaching. Young people have all sorts of *desires,* and a great many of them are *evil,* but then older people have evil desires too. The kind of passion which is in Paul's mind is the kind often seen in young Christian leaders, which is inappropriate and doubly inappropriate in a man of Timothy's standing. It might be his reluctance to shoulder the responsibility that comes with age, to act as if all the problems were not really his problem, or perhaps an impetuosity, a willingness to divide over minor issues. Or it may have been personalising issues so that disagreement with the leader is seen as a mark of being out of step with God. Such attitudes are unhelpful in a church already deeply divided on personal and theological issues, and Timothy must not pour petrol on the fire.

Instead he is to *pursue righteousness, faith, love and peace.* Having told Timothy what to *flee* he now tells him what to follow, and it is the normal route of Christian maturity. There is nothing particular for him here as a Christian leader, and perhaps that is the lesson. Just because he is a pastor does not excuse him from being a Christian. He must handle his opponents and their teaching with Christian maturity.

Friendliness

In a divided church there is a grave danger for a Christian leader in thinking that there are precious few Christians left in the congregation; indeed, there may only be one. So Paul reminds Timothy that he is to pursue Christian maturity *along with those who call on the Lord out of a pure heart.* There will almost certainly be others who will share his concern for the church; he is to seek them out and spend time with them. Isolationism is a great danger for a worried pastor.

Discernment

Once Timothy begins to engage with the teaching ministry again, he will discover what every pastor discovers, that there is no end to the variety of errors in the church for which he is responsible. He will have to learn which are the serious ones, which need root and branch action, and which are the ones that involve him in *foolish and stupid arguments,* which can only *produce quarrels.* Paul's advice is *Don't have anything to do with* them. There will be times in his ministry when he must leave a daft comment unchallenged, and simply move the discussion on.

Kindness

Rather than responding quickly and too sharply, Timothy must remember that his character is as much under scrutiny as the teaching itself, and it is imperative that *the Lord's servant must not quarrel. He must be kind to everyone,* especially the silly ones who are going after the latest fad to come to town. Kindness must mark Timothy's manner exactly at the point where it will be most tested, where he is dealing with people who disagree with him. All too often Christian leaders ignore this command, and concentrate on winning arguments at the expense of losing people. It is quite possible to be doctrinally right but relationally wrong (1 Corinthians 13:2).

Credibility

Timothy must be reluctant to engage in trivial arguments, but that does not mean he should avoid issues of truth and falsehood; rather, his attitude towards people should earn him the right to be heard, and he must be *able to teach.* The point is less about Timothy's doctrinal accuracy or communicative gift than that he must not abuse his position as a teacher so that people will not learn from him. The characteristics either side of this are to do with relationships rather than abilities.

Forgiveness

Continuing the theme of a teacher relating to those with whom he disagrees, Paul tells Timothy he must not be *resentful.* Every conversation has a history, as those involved build on previous conversations and relationships. Where that history has involved conflict, it is all too easy for the past to ease its way into the present. Timothy must make a habit of wiping the slate clean, and not assume that the person who is wrong on one issue is wrong on every issue, nor that because they clashed in the past they are bound to clash on every occasion. This is a hard task for any Christian, let alone a leader who might have been the target of some quite personal attacks, but Paul insists that it should be done. Indeed, he models it when he speaks of the betrayal of various Christians and adds *May it not be held against them* (4:16).

Humility

Because Timothy has been taught and trained by Paul, and because he has known the scriptures from his youth, he knows a great deal – probably a great deal more than his opponents. It would be all too easy for him to ridicule them, humiliate them in front of others, and generally make life unpleasant. Every Christian leader has felt the temptation to crush an irritating church member by displaying just a little bit more knowledge. Such condescension is to be far from Timothy's mind, because *Those who oppose him he must gently instruct,* taking the time and trouble to help them to a better understanding.

Courage

But that will not mean an easy life for him, because although Timothy's manner is to be marked by gentleness, his task is to *instruct,* which does imply that he is the teacher, they the pupils, he the knowledgeable one and they the ignorant or misguided. So for all the stress on relationships, Paul is not telling Timothy to avoid teaching that might lead to conflict. Rather, because truth and love are cut from the same cloth, he needs to keep both together. Truth without love has ceased to be truth; love without truth has ceased to be love.

Optimism

Timothy's ministry is to be marked by a knowledge that because any conversion is God's initiative, and any understanding of the truth comes from God's teaching, even his hardhearted and often empty-headed opponents are not beyond redemption. Every step of the way, in every conversation and teaching opportunity, he is to work on the assumption that it is *in the hope that God will grant them repentance leading to a knowledge of the truth.*

It is all too easy to think that some people are completely unteachable and will never understand. The truth is that none of us can become Christian or abandon false teaching unless God grants us repentance, and if it is in his gift then no false teacher is potentially beyond change. We should pray for those who publicly oppose the gospel, even when they do so from a background of having once believed it. God can *grant … repentance* to the most stubborn of sinners and make them *come to their senses* – after all, he granted it to each one of us.

Realism

Yet Timothy should realise what he is facing. These people are sinning, which is why he is to work towards their *repentance*, and they are stupid, which is why they need to *come to their senses*. But behind the sin and stupidity lies Satan, *who has taken them captive to do his will*. There are numerous ways to translates these verses, but the NIV is probably right here: the devil has taken them captive to do his (that is, the devil's) will.

There is a supernatural agent behind the issues of false teaching and defection from the gospel, and it is his plan to corrupt as many Christians and as much teaching as possible. By the simple expedient of persuading people that God's promise is actually a lie, and hope for the future needs to be redefined as merely an alternative description of the present, he has achieved his plan of making professing Christians destroy one another's faith (2:18).

This list of characteristics of *the Lord's servant* describes the kind of person who will be able to engage in the arduous task of being a Christian leader. It is a demanding catalogue, but nothing less is required by churches if they are to survive what Paul is about to describe as *terrible times* (3:1).

STUDY, DISCUSSION AND PRAYER

1. Which aspect of false teaching do you need to work to remove from your own thinking?

2. Which of the list do you most need to pray about and take action over?
   - Purity
   - Holiness
   - Usefulness
   - Preparedness
   - Maturity
   - Friendliness
   - Discernment

- Kindness
- Credibility
- Forgiveness
- Humility
- Courage
- Optimism
- Realism

3. Pray!

21

Godlessness in the Last Days

3:1–5

In chapter 2 Paul has given Timothy careful instructions on how to handle the tricky issue of remaining personally pure in an impure church, and how to lead those who are tempted into immorality. The focus thus far has been on encouraging Timothy to stand fast. Now Paul lifts the curtain on the wider church scene and shows more of the context that led to Timothy having such troubles. He was among Christians dangerously open to the influence of a poisonously anti-Christian culture. Some of the leaders and congregations have even moved away from Paul, and begun actively recruiting for their version of Christianity. Their apparent success was what was beginning to cause Timothy to have doubts about the effectiveness of his own ministry.

TWO AGES

According to the old saying, the whole world is divided into two groups: those who divide the world into two groups, and those who do not. It is a neat little puzzle, but points to a truth about Christians. We are definitely in the group that divides the world into two.

The Bible makes frequent divisions. Sometimes it compares people racially (Jew, Gentile) or spiritually (in Adam, in Christ). That same division might be put geographically, as John does in Revelation when he says we are either inhabitants of Jerusalem or Babylon, described as the bride or the prostitute. Here, Paul makes his division along the lines of time, when he talks about *the last days*.

Hebrews 1:1 shows the background to this more clearly: *In the past God spoke to our forefathers through the prophets at many times and in various ways, but in these last days he has spoken to us by his Son.* The division in human time occurs because of Jesus. And it is no mere chronological distinction, before Christ and after Christ, but a declaration that Jesus has brought about a promised new phase of God's relationship with humans. In Jesus' earthly ministry he said and did things which people had normally expected would mark the end of the world. He rewrote the Old Testament law and claimed a higher authority than Moses, David or any of the prophets. He healed the disabled and included the outcasts. He announced the end of the Exile from God's presence in Jerusalem, and the start of a new kingdom that would include Gentiles. But above all, he was raised from the dead.

Resurrection of all of humanity was a hope that Old Testament believers had in some measure, and they believed that it would mark the end of the world. It was to be a time of great celebration, God's Year, of the Day of the Lord. So when Jesus is raised from the dead, and is installed as God's delegated judge, it proves that the end of the world has begun. The Last Days have begun. The people who devised our calendar were right to distinguish between BC (Before Christ, God's King), and AD, (Anno Domini, the Year of the Lord). The end of the world began when Jesus was raised from the dead. It was the first day of the Last Days. The day when we shall be raised from the dead will be the last day of the Last Days. So in between the first day of the Last Days and the last day of the Last Days lies where we are today: the Last Days.

That understanding of time is crucial to what Paul says at the start of 2 Timothy 3 – we live in the Last Days. He is not making an obscure prophecy about a point at some distant time when the church will decline irreversibly into error. Rather, because we live in the Last Days we should be doing all the things that Jesus told us to do while we wait. We should be involved in churches that are teaching and evangelising, with a global perspective. That is the appropriate way to respond to the Last Days, and it is what was the focus of both Paul's and Timothy's ministry. The Last Days is another term for the gospel age, and it is a wonderful time to be alive.

So Paul's warning has a bite for all Christians in all times and places: *There will be terrible times in the last days.* He says this as an encouragement, because the knowledge that Jesus' resurrection has inaugurated his kingdom is a heady truth that might lead some people into hyper-enthusiasm where problems are supposed to have no place in a Christian's, or a church's, life. Paul wants to make it clear that we *mark this,* so that we do not become too discouraged when difficulties come. All Christians live in the Last Days, by definition, and some of us will have to live through terrible times.

TERRIBLE TIMES

Timothy obviously lived in a *terrible time,* which is why Paul wrote the description which follows, and it is supposed to make us ask whether we live in a *terrible time* too. What are its characteristics? How can I survive it? How can the church I am part of survive it? And how can we ensure that there are authentic Christians into the next generation and beyond?

It is a long list, which it is hard to divide up well. There may be a hint of the ten commandments in the phrase *disobedient to parents.* But to see the list most clearly there are two points to notice.

First, the list starts as if Paul is talking about society in general (*people* ...) but ends with a clear focus on the church, and especially its leaders (*having a form of godliness but denying its power* ... followed by a description of pseudo-evangelism). In between it is a rather peculiar and mixed description. It could be a party political manifesto from the opposition on what is wrong with the consequences of the government's policies, or a call for a new moral agenda for the nation. It could even be a report from a church group on the world we live in, were it not for that peculiar endpoint of church leadership. In fact, far from being a report on the world from the church it is actually a report on the worldliness of the church. The reason we find it hard to look at the list and see where the world ends and the church begins, is that Paul had exactly the same problem with the church he was describing. He couldn't see where Ephesus stopped and the Ephesian Christians began.

This church, says Paul, offers no contrast to its surrounding culture. It has absorbed its values, habits and failings completely, and surrendered to its context.

This becomes even clearer with the second point, which is that although it is difficult to see a flow in Paul's list, perhaps because he drew it up randomly, it is not difficult to see an overall shape. It begins with two references to love (*lovers* ... *lovers* ... 2) and ends with two references to love (*lovers* ... *lovers* ... 4), and roughly in the middle there is another description of *lovers* (verse 3), this time in the negative (the phrase *without love* in verse 3 uses a different Greek word to the other references). So Paul has structured his list to make a simple but devastating point: what makes a church fall into terrible times will be what it loves, or what it values. If the motivation of love is removed from the list, everything else he mentions is behaviour. The misplaced loves of the church are the cause of everything else which goes wrong. There are three of them.

Lovers of themselves (verse 2)

In a church such as this, the spotlight will not be on loving God or on loving others, which are the right points for the spotlight to illuminate, but on the individual and his or her needs. The object of worship in this church is the self. A church like this will offer a range of ways for people to worship the self, perhaps by improving self-esteem or focusing on needs and problems. On Sunday mornings people will arrive crushed, tired and bored, and the church's task is to ensure they leave lifted, stimulated and ready to face the next week with energy.

That church will be a great success wherever it starts, and will have a huge drift of members of existing churches to join, and great success with non-Christians who will never be challenged to change at all. They arrive as lovers of self and leave as lovers of self, now strongly encouraged to continue in their idolatry by the message they have heard.

Every Christian is to some degree a worshipper at this church, which is why we have to be commanded to love God and our neighbours as much as we love ourselves. But a church should be a place where that command is sounded, not where it is stifled.

Lovers of money (verse 2)

Money, of course, is power made solid. The cash in our pockets and the money in our banks represent a world of possibilities, and the more money we have the more possibilities we have. By means of this power we can employ the world's finest musicians to record the music we want and play it at our command; we can employ highly trained designers to make clothes and display them at a shop just around the corner. Money in itself is just metal and paper – but if we have enough metal and paper we can fulfil our culture's highest dream, which is to stop working and live on a beach for life.

Christians, of course, reject such thoughts. We know that there are crass versions of Christianity which claim that if Jesus were alive today he would wear a Rolex, and that God wants us to be rich, but we know enough about the Bible and the world to know that such a message must be a sick lie.

Except that we still believe it. Even Christians hanker after the larger house, the newer car, the fancier television, the smarter address, the yacht. Even Christians, who know that their sisters and brothers across the world go to bed hungry at night for the want of the cost of this book, and that Jesus warns about his severe judgment on people like us, love money and construct their churches around it.

We manage to be subtle about it. I am English, and we profess not to like things that are too new or 'flash'. English Christians distrust promises made to their wallets. But our love of money still shows. We like our conference centres to be converted English country houses, and our pastors to have accents that come from expensive private education.

The church where such Christians meet is a pleasant place to be. The building, although old, has been comfortably carpeted and furnished. The Bibles are all new, and the band has the latest PA system. A laptop computer shines the words for the songs on a screen, and the effective lighting system dims subtly to allow them to be seen. The coffee afterwards is good, and there is talk of a cappuccino machine to keep the sophisticated thirty-somethings. If there is a problem it is solved financially.

There is nothing necessarily wrong in any of those things, and soon the laptop projecting song words will look as dated as hand-written OHP sheets do today. But the reason the rest of us will catch up and buy the new technology is because we are all members at such churches. Loving money is so deeply built into our surrounding culture, and we are so affected by that culture, that we do not notice that Sunday by Sunday our meetings are flirting with idolatry.

Potentially, the principal idolaters are church leaders, which is where Paul directs his attack. Our culture is becoming both increasingly godless and increasingly technologically efficient. What more simple temptation for pastors could there be than thinking that the reason we are ineffective is because we do not have the right technology? This last quarter century has seen millions of dollars and pounds, which could have been spent on training and employing an army of evangelists, preachers and church planters, being spent instead on rebuilding, repainting, recarpeting and refurnishing buildings where the lovers of St Money can see their god being worshipped. Most Evangelical Christians are not moved to wonder by a great cathedral or an artist's masterpiece. But perversely, we are more excited by a new carpet than a new convert.

Lovers of pleasure (verse 4)

The keys to the success of this church – and, like the preceding two, it is a highly successful church – is that it repeatedly asks one simple question: What do people like? Initially this is quite innocuous, because it is merely that the elders ask whether people prefer old hymns or new songs, whether they shift in their seats after fifteen minutes of the sermon, and enquire after newcomers' first impressions. They notice, and respond to, answers like 'There are plenty of people like me', or 'I liked the children's talk because I could understand it'. They are suitable questions for the elders to ask, and common replies. No one would dream that the elders might make godless decisions that might be based on people's love of pleasure.

Taken further, our culture might place two more pressures on the church. The first is that any information should be packaged as entertainment, and the closer the Christian teaching can be to the style and level of a TV chat show the better. The chat show is a non-demanding format – it is designed to be pleasant and to appeal to lovers of pleasure. The pastor should expect to have to move in that direction. The second demand is that there should be no demand which requires people to stop doing what they enjoy doing, because the enjoyability of something is its highest justification. That an act feels good or right defines it as being good or right – and that is at the heart of being a lover of pleasure. A church that follows this route will find it increasingly difficult to show how its members are different from the surrounding culture, because at any point where the members might have to choose between pleasure and Christ, the church capitulates. This has clearly been the case over sexual morality in our generation, but it should not be limited there. The fact that it is acceptable in Evangelical circles for Christians to change churches merely because of the quality of the band shows that we are deeply implicated in being lovers of pleasure.

AN UNHOLY TRINITY

Self, money and pleasure are an unholy trinity which displace the real God in his church, because they are loved *rather than God* (verse 4). Those who worship self will not worship the God whose true worshipper says *join with me in suffering for the gospel* (1:8). Those who worship money and all the glitz it supplies will not be among those who are *not ashamed of ... chains* (1:16). Those who worship pleasure will find it impossible to *flee the evil desires of youth* (2:22). They will not want to be in a church that is full of the Holy Spirit, because they are too entranced by the Spirit of the Age.

Paul has one final point about the people who set up churches like these, and in many ways it is the most alarming. They operate *having a form of godliness but denying its power* (verse 5). That is, they set up the false churches using the right kind of language and engaging in the right kind of activity, and their congregations are in such terrible danger precisely because the error which is taught sounds so close to the truth, but it lacks *power.* According to 1:8, *power* in this letter means the God-given ability to hold fast to the truth and continue to act on it in Christian leadership, even when the price for such obedience is almost impossibly high.

The three false churches fail at this point, because they all deny that there is any need to stand out in the way Paul suggests. There is no need to avoid the behaviour list in these verses, and so Christians do not need God's help to do so. Churches and their leaders need not be rebuked for their pride, greed or any of the other characteristics Paul describes because those are the ways the world operates and so they are how these churches operate. The traits may not be present in full strength in the churches, but they will be present in some form or other. The reason goes to the heart of the whole theme of suffering for the gospel throughout this letter: it is because these churches have removed the cross from the centre of their activities that all their church-like activities can continue and prosper, because the note of demand has disappeared. They even engage, as the next section will show, in evangelism which replaces the cross with technique. *Have nothing to do with them.*

STUDY, DISCUSSION, AND PRAYER

1. What difference should it make that we know we live in the last days?

2. Do you think we live in what Paul means by *terrible times*?

3. Which of the three loves is of greatest danger to you?

4. Can you identify any trends in your church motivated by love of self, money or pleasure?

5. Are there any other items on the list which are a particular concern today?

22

Godless ministry in the Last Days

3:6–9

The churches and leaders Paul described are not a hypothetical game for Timothy. He experienced genuine heartache as he saw his precious church members being deceived into false churches by false gospels. Paul now outlines their evangelistic strategy, not just to show the disastrous consequences of their false mission, methods and message, but to provide a dark contrast to his own practice, and what he hopes will be Timothy's.

Their strategy is a simple three-step one: they target the vulnerable, tell them what they want to hear, and involve them in a never-ending but fruitless study course. The vulnerable are the *weak-willed women,* not called weak-willed because they were women, but because some of them were at home and were particularly gullible and suitable for the visiting program. These people choose their prey carefully. The tragedy is that these women need to hear the gospel, because they are *loaded down with sins and swayed by all kinds of evil desires.* Ironically they have encountered the very false churches that cannot help them because their message panders to those desires. They certainly have a message because there will be an intensive course of *learning* for these new disciples, even though the true end point of understanding the gospel, *the truth,* will never be reached.

There are several lessons here. The first is that not everyone doing evangelism offers the gospel, and that it is possible to grow a church that converts people without converting them to the truth. It is not enough for a person to be converted. These women have been converted to a lie.

The second lesson is that churches which are concerned with evangelism in the way Paul means it will find themselves opposed by the quasi-churches in the same way that Paul himself was opposed and that *Jannes and Jambres opposed Moses* (3:8). Those were the names traditionally given to the leaders of the rebellion against Moses in Numbers 16. It is a mistake to think that engaging in evangelism will mean not having to be involved in battles against false teaching. We will have to point out to people what the false gospels are which might convert them instead.

Thirdly, we need to see what the quasi-churches are truly like rather than believing them to be as successful as they appear. Paul says their character is *depraved* (verse 8), that God's verdict on them is that they are *rejected* (verse 8), and the most encouraging note for Timothy is that they are temporary, because *they will not get very far* (verse 9). The terrible times will come to an end, and the churches that have fallen for the *folly* will wake up to reality.

STUDY, DISCUSSION AND PRAYER

1. Can you identify groups or churches that operate with a false mission, methods or message in your area?

2. How can you make sure your church does not become like this, or that you do not become trapped by such methods?

3. Which suspect groups regularly come to your door? How can you prepare for their next visit? How can you help your friends not to fall into their trap?

4. Pray that God would enlighten these false teachers with the truth of his gospel.

23

Paul's ministry in the Last Days

3:10–13

At the beginning of chapter three Paul gave a list describing the values and behaviour of the rival churches that were undermining Timothy; in verses 10–13 he gives an alternative list, this time of his own values and behaviour. Just as the rival churches' actions produced a rival ministry in verses 6–9, so his values produce a description of his own message, methods and ministry. This section is a clear and intentional contrast between Paul and the rivals, which Timothy is to apply to himself.

Timothy is the character in the middle who can observe and judge both models. It is not just that Paul outlines what he calls *my teaching*, but that Timothy is personally acquainted with this and can judge whether Paul is giving a true account of himself. So there is a double contrast here. Not only is Paul comparing himself to the rivals, but he implicitly compares Timothy to those rivals, and thus subtly draws him alongside.

Quite often a sentence contains one word which is its key. In these verses that one word is 'my' – *my teaching, my way of life, my purpose* (verse 10) – which occurs only once in the Greek but is clearly meant to govern the entire list and not just the first three items. It would be correct to carry on in the same vein: *my faith, my patience, my love* and so on.

Since this is a list, it is appropriate to take each point as it comes and try to relate it to its wider context in the letter as a whole.

FOUR CONTROLLING AIMS

My teaching

Paul has mentioned already the importance of staying close to the teaching he has passed on because of his authority as God's *herald ... apostle and ... teacher* (1:11). It is this shape that Timothy must pass on (1:13) to suitably qualified teachers (2:2). The rivals have a different message (2:18).

My way of life

This is an unusual word which only occurs here in the New Testament. It means something like a line of argument, a way of proving something, a style or orientation. Presumably Paul wants Timothy to remember how he saw Paul start churches from scratch in contrast to the abusive methods of the others.

My purpose

Paul's aim or target was always clear. God's *purpose* (1:9) is the fulfilment of all the promises he had made in the gospel, and Paul's purpose as apostle to the Gentiles was that all the world should hear about God's plan. Paul was driven by a passion for God's glory, which was in complete contrast to the self-motivated and self-targeted churches so worrying Timothy.

My faith

Faith, that is, in the face of hardship. Faith that keeps a clear hope in God and his gospel when the churches seem to be deserting it. Faith when, alone and ill-equipped, he faced the opposition of Rome. And the faith that Timothy now needs in his tough times (1:13).

THREE ATTITUDES TOWARDS PEOPLE

My patience

Paul knew what it was to be deeply disappointed by fellow Christian workers (1:15), deeply irritated by their betrayal (2:17), and deeply hurt by opposition (4:14). But he manages to take a long-term view on these things. His quarrel over John Mark had faded to some extent (Acts 15:37–39, cf 2 Timothy 4:11) and the malicious Alexander will be rebuked by God, not Paul (4:14). Timothy is to show similar patience as a teacher (2:25, 4:2), even when people appear unwilling to learn the truth and are gullible towards error.

My love

When Paul was undergoing hardship for the sake of others, whether he was their leader or their fall-guy, it would have been easy to let resentment build. But his perspective on the gospel and its ultimate truth means he was willing to undergo anything if that meant others becoming Christians (2:10). Timothy must show similar gentleness towards those who oppose him (2:25).

My endurance

It is important not to sentimentalise Paul, as if he never experienced discouragement. It is only in the face of such bewilderment and loneliness as 4:16–18 describes that real faith and courage has any meaning. The way to build endurance is by enduring, and the way to learn to endure is if God puts you through the fire over and again.

VARIOUS HEARTBREAKS

All seven of those aims or attitudes are to some extent under Paul's control, but the next part of his list comprises events which are outside his ability to alter. Notice how they shift to the plural, as Paul encountered them time after time.

Paul is being deliberately general here, although *persecutions* are clearly originating with people, whether officials, false teachers, or organised thugs, and *sufferings* is a more widely descriptive term for earthquakes, storms at sea, shipwrecks and the like. Paul expected these circumstances precisely because he was an apostle (1:12). He draws Timothy's attention to some he would have known about because of meeting Paul on the first great missionary journey, involving Antioch (Acts 13:48–52, 14:19–21), Iconium (Acts 14:1–5,19) and Lystra (Acts 14:21). Paul's first missionary journey had foreshadowed all the others by being a time of great hardship (14:22).

But, still he stood as an evangelist, apostle and leader. He had been whipped, beaten and he was still in chains, but his concern was to have *finished the race* (4:7).

There are two lessons here, one for Timothy and one for, or about, the false teachers.

PAUL'S EXPERIENCE WAS NOT UNIQUE (VERSE 12)

Timothy needs to know that his experience is not unique either, so he was not allowed to excuse himself from defending the gospel because he found it hard or other people opposed him. Timothy was normal. Calvin says in his sermon on this section, 'We must be ready to go not only when the way lies clear before us, but to take hedge and ditch, and go on forwards through brambles and briars; for such is the condition of the faithful and of all the children of God'. Opting out of contending for the faith because it is difficult is not an acceptable excuse. Paul is not saying that this situation of persecution applies to all Christians permanently and equally, but that when such times come we must be willing to stand.

IMPOSTORS SHOW APPARENT SUCCESS (VERSE 13)

Paul has already shown that there are *evil* (3:2–5) *impostors* (3:6–9); now he adds to their character, their future. They will indeed make progress as they claim, but it will only be progress into increasing moral perversion. Their progress has a price, because although they start out by lying to others, they end up believing the lies other people tell them. We should not be surprised that when people are unmasked as frauds they show considerable indignation. Their chosen path means that they so surround themselves with lies to keep up the facade of success and blessing that they become incapable of telling truth from error.

STUDY, DISCUSSION AND PRAYER

1. Which of the items in Paul's list is the greatest challenge for you?

2. Pray about what specifically makes you reluctant to be identified as a Christian.

3. Identify some areas where the Christian church today is in danger of believing lies, and pray for their leaders.

24

Timothy's ministry in the Last Days

3:14–17

These verses contain probably the most famous words in the whole letter, and among the most famous in the New Testament. In them, Paul gives a ringing endorsement of the truth that all the Bible, Old Testament as well as New, is to be treated by Christians as God's definitive message to his world. Many helpful books covering the issues around biblical inspiration sensibly begin with, or include at an early stage, a discussion of these important words.

Although these verses have an important function in describing the Bible's view of the Bible, the precise purpose they have here is much more narrow, however broad the implications. One danger in reading the Bible without first noticing what verses like these are saying in their context is that their power is somehow diminished.

Paul is continuing his challenge to Timothy to be loyal: having described the false ministries in rival churches, and reminding Timothy of what he knew about Paul, Timothy's own ministry comes under scrutiny. It is a continual method in this letter to offer a series of contrasting examples (1:8, 15–16 etc). Now Timothy is invited to measure himself against Paul, and see if he passes the test for loyalty. But how could he tell if he had passed? What criteria would satisfy such a piercing critic as Paul?

Timothy is not alone in this review of his ministry. In Paul's sights are the congregation who have remained with Timothy, the congregation who have left, and the potential future leaders and teachers. A great deal depends upon Timothy remaining loyal to Paul, not merely in his doctrine but in his practice of ministry.

The main concern is summed up in verse 14: *continue in what you have learned and become convinced of,* which is another key verse to a correct understanding of the whole letter. Timothy is to continue in the pattern which he heard, understood, and was persuaded to live by as a church leader. That pattern he gained from Paul, the countless church planting colleagues whom he had observed Paul train, and the countless church leaders who had had the lessons about the nature of ministry drilled into them by Paul. He is to continue not just because it is true (although it is) but because Paul's ministry exemplified the truth that ministry is tough by definition and that it requires determination to continue in it. He is to continue not only in the truth of the gospel, but in the truth that church leaders suffer for the gospel, and that it is the shape of true Christian ministry as well as the shape of true Christian doctrine which must be passed on. He needs to keep to what he has learned because there are so many winsome alternatives around which do not require the Christian worker to suffer. Then as now, the longer someone remains in Christian ministry the more attractive become the alternatives. Timothy as a young man signed up to work with Paul with hardly a thought; Timothy as an older man is beginning to find the price a high one.

Timothy's resources, both as a Christian and as a leader, are the same: the *Scriptures.* If they are correctly understood, taught and applied to all of his life and ministry, they will lead him and keep him in salvation in Christ. They will equip him for the kind of ministry God wants him to have. If that sounds too slick, remember the fierce debates that Timothy was having (or possibly avoiding having) on the resurrection; the quarrels and arguments that time-wasters want to draw him into; those gullible shut-ins who are *always learning but never able to acknowledge the truth.* Timothy's confidence has been severely rocked, and it would be dangerous for him if he felt that he could no longer rely on the Bible as a resource for his ministry because the trouble makers have hijacked it and used it for their own advantage. Paul has had to reassure and rebuke Timothy on this point earlier (2:14–15), but this time his point is tighter. The Scriptures are not an unsupervised playground where anyone can prove what they like – they are written and given by God with the end result of saving people. Timothy can be confident that they will do God's work for him as he handles them in his ministry, week by week. That is what those famous verses are about. They are not here to prove the doctrine of inspiration (although they do, and it is an important doctrine), nor do they prove the usefulness of the Scriptures (which is closer to what Paul meant); rather, they reassure Timothy and all flagging ministers of the adequacy of the scriptures to accomplish the work God has given them.

It is worth taking these familiar words slowly, in order to hear what Paul is saying.

All Scripture ...

Paul has reminded Timothy already of his debt to his mother and grandmother for teaching him the *holy Scriptures* (1:5) by bringing him up as a Jew. Once again the idea of taking his turn in responsible leadership is underlined for him. *Scripture,* of course, would have meant what we call the Old Testament, although it is tempting to think that Paul is combining what he has just called *holy Scripture* with the Christian teaching Timothy had subsequently *learned and ... become convinced of* (verse 14), to form the composite idea of *all Scripture.* More obviously, though, Paul is reassuring him that all the Old Testament is suitable material for the Christian teacher to base his ministry on, and he does not have to retreat from those parts that the rival churches have made their own. It is quite striking today that after generations of writers and teachers making this verse the foundation for countless books, conferences and statements of doctrine, Christian confidence in handling the Old Testament is still embarrassingly weak, and restricted to a few well-known passages. Paul wanted to give back to Timothy an entire Bible. Perhaps he would wish to give it back to us as well.

... is inspired by God ...

Those who use this verse in their defence of a verbal inspiration of the Bible are right to do so. These words are crucial not only for this letter but because they are one of the clearest expressions of the Bible's origin and authority to be found in the Bible. They are a battleground today.

First, we should note that the word translated *inspired* is more accurately 'expired', or 'breathed out'. The distinction is important because of the way we easily talk of a great work of art or brilliant human being as 'inspired'. That casual way of thinking has its roots deep in secular Western thought, with various intellectual movements that have been fundamentally opposed to Christianity. The Romans would talk of the *genius* of a place or a person, meaning some abiding presence or power, and they would visit a grave or a temple to gain some renewed vision. That idea reappeared in the eighteenth century with the Romantic movement, and has never really died away. The likes of Beethoven or Napoleon were seen as touched with some kind of genius, and people today still visit their homes and graves to touch and recapture their spirits. Part of the whole Romantic vision was the idea of the wild and untamed world being inspired, and it drove artists into the wildernesses of Europe, America, Australia and the deserts of Arabia, and plunged poets into drug-fuelled excess. It was a fundamentally pagan movement, and it is still around. It is the reason that people pay vast sums for the piano on which John Lennon composed 'Imagine', and try to find God up a mountain or on a beach.

The words 'inspired' or 'inspiring' are sometimes used of the Bible in that sense too. It is treated as one of the great treasures of literature, and its very passion and faith can make even an agnostic or atheist feel stronger, because it shows how great humans can be.

Of course, the reverse is true – the Bible shows how great God is, and how stupid and weak humans are. The word 'expired' captures that well, because it shows the direction in which the Bible has travelled. It has its origin with God and has come from him to us.

There is also an intimate connection between breathing out and speaking. We can speak because our breath passes over our vocal cords, and God speaks because his breath creates his Word. That is because in both the Old and New Testaments the word 'breath' is the same one used for his 'Spirit'. God has spoken his words to us by the work of the Holy Spirit in producing our Bibles. It is a grand statement to call the Bible 'God's Word', but it is a true one.

We speak for two reasons, either to make ourselves known or to make some information known, and that is why God speaks to us too. Because of sin we are both estranged from him and ignorant about him. But in his mercy God has spoken so that we can know him in both senses: he allows us to have a loving relationship with him (that is, we know him) on the basis of knowing and believing the truth about him. He has spoken to draw us into a loving relationship of truth. It is fundamental to the idea of God in the Bible that he is a God who speaks. He created and upholds the universe by his word (Genesis 1:3, Hebrews 1:3), and he will destroy, judge and save by means of the same word (2 Peter 3:5–9). Whether it is by promise, law, covenant, prophecy or gospel, the common factor in all is that God speaks, and all the rival idols of our day are ludicrously dumb.

Because it is obvious that ordinary people, like Paul, wrote the Bible for other ordinary people, like Timothy, and that they did it consciously and with different styles, it is right to talk about the 'double authorship' of the Bible. As Peter puts it, *men spoke from God as they were carried along by the Holy Spirit* (2 Peter 1:21). There must equally be two parts to our understanding: we need to work at our study and understanding, and we need to pray that God will give us that understanding. As Paul has already told Timothy, *Reflect on what I am saying, for the Lord will give you insight into all this* (2:7).

A necessary consequence of the Bible's inspiration is its continuing authority. A Christian will not only read the Bible for understanding but must put it into practice. To know what to do and fail to do it is as rebellious as refusing to listen in the first place. Jesus warned, *Why do you call me 'Lord, Lord,' and do not do what I say?* (Luke 6:46) and that warning is repeated throughout the Bible. It tells us that the basic response of the Christian to God is one of submission, of saying he is right and we are wrong – which is the exact opposite of the rebellion in the garden. If we go wrong here we will inevitably go wrong elsewhere. Refusal to believe that God means what he says is a guarantee that one will drift disastrously far from him.

There are constant rivals to God's claim over us, and we need to be on our guard. For some it is the strength of their experiences, for others it is the power of their intellect; it might be the centuries of Christian tradition, or the latest results of the social sciences. Experience of other cultures and religions causes believers to question the truth-claims of Christianity, even though both Testaments were born in pluralist and pagan settings and are not surprised by them. Some people think it is ignorant and naive to say that what God said then, in a pre-scientific age, is what he still says today. They suggest that God is moving on today in what he is saying, beyond what he has said before, opening up new truths that before were closed to previous generations. The irony is that each generation thinks exactly that. In the 1500s people began to speak of the rebirth (or Renaissance) of classical culture that had been lost in the Christian 'Middle Ages'; in the 1700s others talked of an Enlightenment following the darkness of Europe believing the Bible. Our culture has a marked preference for the *avant garde* (literally, the advance guard), and it is the ultimate defence of a shocking play, film or novel that every true artist has been derided by the (usually Christian) powers-that-be. That is an easily disproved lie, but it has proved a useful one in the hands of those who have tried to subvert Christianity.

Sadly, since Christians are deeply worldly, that same fascination with the new infiltrates our churches. The assumption that God is doing a new thing today is widespread, even though what we identify as the new thing differs widely. For some it is a change in sexual morality, for others a shift from belief to emotion as the centre of assurance, for yet others a new 'word' from God about the next revival. Frequently that fascination is justified by the growing idea that God does not know the future, and is delighted or saddened by the new things that occur. All betray a common discomfort with the idea that God has already said what he intends to say, in full knowledge of what questions might be raised today, and our part is to believe.

Sociologists sometimes talk of the 'plausibility structure' of society, which means that every culture sees some things as evidently true and not worth arguing about, and some as evidently false and not worth considering. That is why Christians find it hard within themselves and their churches to drum up enthusiasm for evangelism. The idea that one religion might claim to be the only way to God, and that its believers might act as if that claim were true, is deeply implausible in our cultural setting, and every TV soap, newspaper and blockbuster novel will underline that feeling. Our unease about the Bible's authority needs to be countered, and the only way will be for churches to become alternative 'plausibility structures', where God and his truth claims are treated as self-evidently true, and the intellectual framework of our surrounding culture demonstrated to be self-serving and inconsistent. Whichever culture we live in that will always be the challenge, because every way of thinking about God, ourselves and our world that does not begin with God speaking authoritatively to us in the Bible is doomed to failure. We cannot engage with the world by letting it set our agenda. God has spoken and still speaks the same word. We need to take that inspired and authoritative message into our world so that God will draw ignorant and distant men and women into a saving relationship as they believe his word.

As Timothy had discovered, that also means taking that inspired and authoritative word into the heart of an error prone church. He needs to be reminded that he can have confidence in the Bible to do God's work because it is God's appointed tool for that purpose.

Timothy's task is to make sure he uses the Bible correctly so that God's voice is heard in the church he pastors. The famous four tasks follow: *teaching, rebuking, correcting, and training in righteousness.* The first and last are positive, the middle two are negative, which perhaps shows Timothy that there should not only be a balance between the positive and negative elements in his teaching, but also that the tone that people should be left with is the encouraging one. Timothy is not to be a nag. It is also possible to put the four in a chain: once he has taught the truth he needs to rebuke the error, he then needs to correct it, and then help people reorder their lives and think afresh in the light of the truth. By sticking at any one of the first three points our own handling of the Bible will be respectively bland, irrelevant or moralising.

These verses have an ever sharper edge when they are placed firmly in the setting not merely of Timothy's being a pastor, but of his being a pastor in trouble.

Why does Timothy need to teach?

Because he pastors an ignorant church where the members believe half-truths and even lies. God wants his people to think rightly about him, and so he has appointed those who will explain his ways to them. It is not a harsh criticism of that church to describe it as ignorant: every church is ignorant because it is made up of ignorant Christians like you and me, who do not naturally know anything about God, and without the constant reminding of good Bible teachers will drift off into ignorance again.

Why does Timothy need to rebuke?

Because he pastors an error-ridden church. This task is much harder than the first, because it takes enormous courage to point out that certain teachings are wrong. From the way that Paul mentions Hymenaeus and Philetus, perhaps he wants to encourage him to point out that certain teachers are wrong too. Obviously there is little point sounding off about errors that come nowhere near the congregation. A famous cartoon shows a preacher declaiming to a congregation of two, 'I know what you're thinking: Sabellianism!' But where there is a serious error being believed in the congregation, the Bible is there to command Timothy to rebuke it, and to equip him in that difficult task. (For all the oddity of its name, Sabellianism has been one such error, teaching that God is by turns Father, Son or Holy Spirit, and Christians had to rebuke Sabellius and his followers severely. Their efforts remain in our creeds.)

Why does Timothy need to correct?

Because he pastors a potentially immoral church, attracted away from the true gospel by their love of self, money and pleasure into all kinds of godless behaviour (3:1–5). He needs to show people not only what to believe but how to live. Combating selfishness can be every bit as explosive as combating error.

Why does Timothy need to train people in righteousness?

Because the next generation of Christians and their leaders need to have a pattern of belief and behaviour which is opposed to their culture and desires at almost every point. Recent converts need to have the implications of Christian discipleship spelt out for them clearly and simply. More mature Christians need to have it pointed out to them that they are perhaps much more influenced by their secular setting than they might think.

Timothy is facing a number of battles as a church leader; on some he is forced to be reactive (rebuking, correcting), on others Paul encourages him to be proactive (teaching, training in righteousness). The problem is Timothy's fear. Paul has reassured him that just as the Holy Spirit has equipped him to be reliable (1:7) so the Holy Scriptures have equipped him to teach others. He has been *thoroughly equipped for every good work.*

THE MAN OF GOD

All the way through this section it has been assumed that *man of God* equals pastor, rather than just any Christian. The Old Testament roots for that phrase show that *man of God* was a general term for a prophet, and is used specifically for Moses (Deuteronomy 33:1), David (Nehemiah 12:36) and Elijah (1 Kings 17:24). Paul's use of the term in 1 Timothy 6:11 seems to support the idea that man of God was one of his titles for a Christian leader, and it speaks powerfully of the need for such people to have the word of God in their mouths. In Timothy's time there was not the ready access to portions of the Bible that we enjoy today. Only a privileged few were able to study it and there would have been great attentiveness as it was both read and explained. Our easy familiarity with the Bible should not make us dull to what Paul says here about its God-given right to rule us, nor about the authority, qualifications and responsibility of those who teach God's word in our churches.

STUDY, DISCUSSION AND PRAYER

1. Which parts of *all Scripture* do you see being downplayed in the wider Christian scene?

2. Which parts are you most tempted to downplay?

3. Identify one area where the Bible is at work in you and your church, for Paul's four works of the Bible:
   - Teaching
   - Rebuking
   - Correcting
   - Training in righteousness

For leaders:

Do the same exercise for the various parts of your work. How could every part of your work be a way of exercising a ministry of teaching God's word?

25

The big picture

4:1

CHAPTER 4

The final section of Paul's letters often contains three features which strike the contemporary reader as unusual, but which can help in understanding them. First, there is often an abrupt change of mood, which can confuse us and make us think we have stumbled into another letter by mistake (for example, Romans 12:1, 1 Corinthians 15:1). Second, the main theme of the letter is often repeated, sometimes quite briefly (for example, Romans 16:25–27, Galatians 6:12–16). Third, there may be an extended section of personal greetings which are still relevant because they are in line with the letter's theme. For example, Romans 15 forges links with a church Paul is shortly intending to meet for the first time; 1 Corinthians 16 maintains links between other churches and the increasingly arrogant and isolationist Corinthians; Colossians 4 turns an introspective church outwards as Paul provides fuel for their prayer about evangelism.

Those three factors can be put to work on 2 Timothy 4, which can seem to be an anticlimax. The letter can appear to be winding down from verse 9, and some might think that the authoritative part is over by verse 8, or even verse 5.

But Paul introduces people here for one eighth of the letter, which is quite a large amount, and in view of the way he has written so far it is difficult to categorise this section simply as 'personal remarks'.

It is better to identify 4:1 as introducing a major new section, which means it does not need to be forced to follow on precisely from 3:17. In 4:1 there are four elements: the reality of God's *presence*, that Jesus Christ is the *judge*, and that Timothy should be exercising his ministry in the light of Jesus' *appearing* and *kingdom*. Together they are the context in which Paul's solemn call to loyalty is delivered. The first sign that these elements are important for understanding the structure of the chapter comes in 4:8: *Now there is in store for me the crown of righteousness, which the Lord, the righteous* ***Judge****, will award to me on that day – and not only to me, but also to all who have longed for his* ***appearing****.* Two of the four elements reappear. A third comes in 4:17: *But the Lord stood at my side and gave me strength, so that through me the message might be fully proclaimed and all the Gentiles might hear it. And I was delivered from the lion's mouth. The Lord will rescue me from every evil attack and will bring me safely to his heavenly* ***kingdom****. To him be glory for ever and ever. Amen.* Although the fourth element, God's *presence*, is not described using the same word, it is clear that God's loyalty to Paul as he stood *at my side* is an important issue.

That gives the whole of chapter 4 a coherence, because 4:1–18 now becomes one section divided into two parts, framed by Paul's words about the future. It also leads to the satisfying conclusion that the letter proper ends with a climactic *Amen*.

So 4:1 is the headline over the whole chapter, reminding Timothy that his life and ministry are conducted under God's permanent eye, with a view both to comfort in the daily battle and God's verdict on his ministry on the last day. This is in line with what Paul has said so far about *that day* (1:12, 1:18 etc) and the sapping of Timothy's energy that comes from the presence of the false teaching (2:18). Timothy is reminded and braced for his work.

STUDY, DISCUSSION AND PRAYER

1. How much does Jesus' return play in your thinking and practice? Is Jesus' return central to the way you plan and prioritise?

2. Identify some areas where you know it has made a difference.

3. Pray about some areas where you know you need to change.

26

Keep your head

4:2–5

In this section there are nine commands, or imperatives; five in verse 2: ***Preach** the Word; **be prepared** in season and out of season; **correct**, **rebuke** and **encourage** – with great patience and careful instruction,* and four in verse 5: *But you, **keep your head** in all situations, **endure** hardship, **do the work** of an evangelist, **discharge** all the duties of your ministry.* In between those two verses are the reasons why Timothy is to do them, giving the explanation for Paul's urgency and understanding of the times.

There are striking similarities between verse 2 and 3:16, with the obvious difference that where 3:16 is a statement, this verse is a series of commands. When Paul says *preach,* the word means to announce like a herald. In his view Timothy has important news which must be delivered to the hearers, however the herald thinks it will be received. It is a public announcement of God's truth, demanding a response.

FOUR SEASONS

That word must also be announced whether the herald feels like declaring it or not, which goes to the heart of *be prepared in season and out season.* By being prepared Paul means being spiritually ready to take God's word on board and obey it, but it is difficult to see whether it is readiness of the speaker or the hearer that Paul has in mind. It is even possible that Paul is making a blanket statement.

Being prepared when both Timothy and the church are *in season* will be a joy for the minister and the people. It is (in most ministers' experience) more rare for the church to be *in season* but if the minister feels *out of season* when it happens, the church will soon succumb to the same malaise. When the church and its minister are both *out of season* there is little hope for either of them and no one will be won for Christ. But the situation that Timothy finds himself in is one that many ministers will identify with: the minister is *in season* but the church is *out of season.* Timothy is keen to teach the truth, but the church is increasingly closing its ears to him and opening its ears to others.

Alternatively, we could read all four possibilities but consider that Paul is referring the receptivity or hostility of our surrounding society to the gospel. Again, that would fit Timothy in this letter. In either context Timothy must learn to find the resources to continue to minister effectively while the indifference of the church and the antipathy of the culture conspire to drain away his enthusiasm. He must learn to conduct his ministry under God's present and future eye. Despite what common sense tells him as he sees fewer people at church each week, and as those few insist on telling him about the attractive church they are about to join, only God's verdict counts in the ultimate evaluation of Timothy's ministry.

So he must *correct* where there are mistaken ideas which need straightening out, *rebuke* where he encounters persistent errors which need rooting out and dealing with. He must *encourage* where there are fragile people in the church who need help in finding their way through the spiritual minefield.

THE MINEFIELD

The reason Paul needs to brace Timothy to stick to his task is precisely because of the enervating effect of his time and place. *The time will come,* says Paul, not making a prediction about a one-off event but a guaranteed distraction in the life of every pastor. This distraction will have four elements by which Timothy will recognise it:

The rejected message

The church will *not put up with sound* (that is, healthy) *doctrine* and *will turn their ears away from the truth.* The gospel has a natural home in the church, and for error to flourish it first needs to uproot the truth. Hence the requirement for Timothy to *preach the word.* Not only is that a necessary antidote to error it is a preventative too, for as long as the gospel is visibly at the centre of a church, error cannot take over. But having blocked the influx of error into his congregation Timothy must watch people seep away to another. A faithful ministry such as his will go through times of appearing dull and lacking in appeal.

The selfish motivation

Timothy should expect to see transparent self-centredness as people set up their new congregations, because everything is driven by what will *suit their own desires.* Teaching which challenges and calls for repentance and change will not be high on their agenda. Rather, they will want ministries of encouragement and support, which will affirm, accept and honour everyone, irrespective of their beliefs or lifestyle.

The responsive ministry

People will flock to where they can hear *what their itching ears want to hear,* and because every preacher loves to speak to a crowd and hates to lose it, they will find no shortage of teachers who will willingly massage their felt needs in this demand-led church. The members and leaders are caught in a sick spiral, where each seeks to earn the other's approval.

The preference for myths

Because their ears itch for anything other than truth, they will be fed, and believe, lies. Lies about God, the Bible, the preachers' experiences (which cannot be authentic because they too have *wandered away from the truth* [2:18]), and about Paul and Timothy. It will distress faithful teachers like Timothy that people who have seemed to be satisfied with true teaching turn so quickly to believing fairy tales.

BUT YOU ...

This fourfold attack would have been extremely demoralising for Timothy, as he lost both his congregation and his leaders. It would also have been extremely tempting as he considered whether to join them and become more evidently successful. So Paul draws a clear line between Timothy and the others. *But you,* he says, must be different and distinct. *You* must not give in or go under. *You,* by contrast, must remain faithful. And he resumes his list of nine commands.

We all imagine that the crisis we are currently in is the worst one in recent memory, if not in the history of the church. So Paul's next instruction is a wise word from an experienced pastor who has seen all sorts of problems come and go: *keep your head.* Literally, he says 'keep sober', meaning that Timothy is not to give in to the intoxicating myths of the popular preachers, nor the heady wine of pessimism and despair. Timothy is to keep a realistic and sober view of the situation.

Being realistic about the times he lives in will not be easy, nor will resisting the pressures of cowardice or compromise, so Paul tells him to *endure hardship.* He knows that the task he is calling Timothy to is not easy.

If Timothy's sober assessment of the situation is that he has lost his church members permanently, what is he to do? Don't panic, says Paul, work hard and start a new congregation, by doing *the work of an evangelist.* Timothy is not to despair even if he has to start again from scratch, because the gospel is still true, and people still need to hear it.

Above all he must not give up at this point. *Discharge all the duties of your ministry* has a feel in English of the range of Timothy's ministry, but in the Greek it means more 'Fully complete your ministry, don't give up, don't quit.'

STUDY, DISCUSSION AND PRAYER

1. Which of the four boxes do you think you/your church/ your society currently occupies? Has it changed over the past few years?

Minister in season, church/society in season	**Minister out of season, church/society in season**
Minister in season, church/society out of season	**Minister out of season, church/society out of season**

2. Where do you think your church/denomination/ society is heading? Do you want to encourage that or change direction?

3. How do you respond to teaching when it is difficult or challenges you?

4. What made you join your current church? Were there elements of that decision which were selfish?

5. Would you change church if the Bible teaching was too close to home or told you things you didn't want to hear?

6. What are the stories going around your circle of friends about how other churches or ministries are being spectacularly blessed? Do you believe them, envy them or ignore them?

For leaders:

Who is your audience? For whose sake do you live a Christian life or study the Bible? Whose approval matters most to you?

27

The end?

4:6–8

There is a genuine sense of Paul having reached the end of a ministry, and expecting the younger man to inherit his mantle. Having compared Timothy with the false teachers and their adherents, he now contrasts Timothy with himself, and the *but you* of verse 5 is answered by the *For I* of verse 6. For Paul, the major battles lie in the past; for Timothy, they lie in the future. But all is not quite as it might seem.

DEPARTURE

Despite attempts to show that Paul is expecting to depart from prison, most commentators continue to see this verse as a reference to Paul's death. What makes that conclusive is in a similar passage (Philippians 1:23) the same word *departure* is used and it clearly means 'to die' in that letter. So Paul is aware that his ministry is drawing to a close and that Timothy is going to have to step up to the line.

But how close is that death? In Philippians 2:17 Paul uses the same imagery of a drink offering being poured out, and there too he speaks about it as a present experience, even though he was nowhere near death at that stage. A *drink offering* was not the blood of a slaughtered animal but some liquid, usually wine, being poured out either onto the ground or over a sacrifice. What the two letters have in common is that they were both written from prison, and that is the clue: being *poured out* is Paul's explanation of how it is that his experience of suffering goes hand-in-hand with people hearing about Jesus. The growth of the church is costly for him, much as a drink offering would be, because throwing away the best wine was an apparent waste of good money, and keeping Paul in prison was a waste of a good apostle. But Paul was willing to pay that price if the result was conversions. The fact that Paul has earlier used this imagery of a milder version of his prison experience, and without any reference to an imminent execution, should alert us to the danger of reading things into this passage. Paul has a reason for thinking that his death might be close, but that is because of what has already happened to him, not what he is about to endure.

THE LONG, HARD RACE

Paul evidently understands that some part of his life is over – but what? He used the imagery of fighting (in a sporting, not a military, sense here) to describe Christian ministry (1 Timothy 6:12) and the demands it makes (1 Timothy 4:8). But to stand at the end of one's life and say *I have fought the good fight, I have finished the race, I have kept the faith* (4:7) could sound dangerously close to bragging unless Paul has a particular *fight*, or wrestling match, in mind.

His particular commission as an apostle was to carry the gospel into the Gentile heartland, into its capital, and bear witness to Rome. When he was first converted this was only partly clear, because Jesus said to Ananias that Paul *is my chosen instrument to carry my name before the Gentiles and their kings and before the people of Israel. I will show him how much he must suffer for my name* (Acts 9:15–16). Even at that stage Paul knew his task would involve testifying at a high social level to Gentiles, and that he would pay a high price for it. Gradually Paul began to develop a plan to visit Rome (Acts 19:21), but it became increasingly clear to him that he will travel there in chains. So Paul saw his ministry having a Gentile focus, and that was crystallised in a journey to

Rome and bearing witness before the Imperial Court. Notice the language he uses to describe this journey: *And now, compelled by the Spirit, I am going to Jerusalem, not knowing what will happen to me there. I only know that in every city the Holy Spirit warns me that prisons and hardships are facing me. However, I consider my life worth nothing to me, if only I may finish the race and complete the task the Lord Jesus has given me – the task of testifying to the gospel of God's grace* (Acts 20:22–24). Paul saw that journey, with its attendant perils and unknown climax as a *race* to be run and a *task* to be undertaken.

If Paul increasingly saw his future trial and testimony in Rome as his God-given *race,* and if by the time of 2 Timothy that trial was already over, it would not be surprising to hear him talk of his race having been finished. He talks of his trial towards the end of 2 Timothy in similar terms: *the Lord stood at my side and gave me strength, so that through me the message might be fully proclaimed and all the Gentiles might hear it* (4:17). He had been given the role of apostle to the Gentiles (Galatians 2:8), and of having the responsibility of speaking to the entire earth (Acts 13:47), and from his prison cell he understands that his testimony in Rome has discharged that trust. It is with a note of relief he can see that his God-given journey to Rome is over.

THE VICTOR'S CROWN

Paul did not buckle under the pressure of the court, or take the easy route when he had to speak, despite all the hardships of 4:14–18. He stood firm. So he can look forward to a different courtroom, with a different judge, a different verdict and, compared to his recent aloneness, a huge crowd standing beside him.

The different courtroom is *the Lord*'s throne room, and in contrast to the corruption and bureaucracy of Rome's legal system, God is a *righteous Judge.* On that occasion Paul can expect a fair trial. And because of the gospel, Paul knows in advance that the verdict on that day will be that he is righteous, so he can say confidently that a *crown of righteousness* is already waiting, being kept *in store for* him. Nor is he on his own, for there will be many others beside him, all receiving their crowns of righteousness too. But we should not miss that allusion to the destructive effect of the false teaching. The crown is for, and only for, *all those who have longed for his appearing.* Hymenaeus, Philetus and those who believed their lies will not be there.

STUDY, DISCUSSION AND PRAYER

1. What major life traumas lie behind you? How did you cope as a Christian?

2. Which crises still lie ahead of you? How can you be as brave as Paul?

3. Pray for Christians in prison for their faith today.

28

Planning

4:9–15

Verses towards the end of Paul's letters which contain lists of names and details of travel plans are usually treated as containing little more than delightful but unimportant details. To those who support the idea that Paul wrote 2 Timothy they carry a convincing note of authenticity, a series of alibis and links which make the letter more plausible. To those who think the letter was not by Paul, they are merely a conventional way of finishing a correspondence, and prove nothing except that the writer knew how to make the letter look as if it had come from Paul. To both groups they are charming but inconsequential.

But if the analysis of chapter 4 suggested above (Section 25) is true, then these remarks are moved from the fringes of the letter to its heart. The themes they cover – desertion, loyalty, opposition and the future – are central to the letter as a whole. What is happening is that Timothy is being required to put his strengthened loyalty to the test – to show that he is not ashamed of Paul by visibly aligning himself with him.

DEMAS

Demas was a Christian who had spent time with Paul as a close colleague during a time of imprisonment (Colossians 4:14). He was no stranger to the issues of hardship which Paul's current circumstances raised. He was also aware of the necessity of doctrinal clarity and truth and the need to battle for it, because Colossians deals with similar issues. And being mentioned in the same breath as Luke means he was in the inner circle of Paul's team. Demas had been a loyal co-worker.

But something had gone tragically wrong, because Demas *has deserted me and has gone to Thessalonica* (4:10), a long way from Rome. Once again, Paul shows that even close colleagues can wilt under pressure and give up their relationship with him.

Demas fled *because he loved this world*, which at least means that he preferred fresh air to dank prisons, and the company of free people rather than the thugs who shared Paul's cell. But in view of what Paul has analysed as problems in the church, two of the words in that reason have particular force. First, the problem with Demas was what he *loved* and Paul has already exposed the power of wrong affections in 3:1–4, where he wrote of *lovers of themselves, lovers of money ... lovers of pleasure rather than lovers of God.* Demas seems to have the same problem as the others Paul described. Secondly, the object of his affections is *this world.* All the way through 2 Timothy Paul has been arguing for a correct understanding of the future in God's plan, and that it is worth suffering here and now in order to have a share in it. For him, that means prison; for Demas, that meant being in known association with Paul. And Demas found the price too high. Because he *loved* (literally, 'has fallen in love with') *this world* rather than the next he was unwilling to suffer in it by close association with Paul. And he left.

It is a warning that even the most loyal workers can find the price of ministry too much.

CRESCENS AND TITUS

So how have these two men fared? About *Crescens* we know nothing except what it says here, although there is a legend he later became a bishop; *Titus* is presumably the same one who was left by Paul in Crete (Titus 1:5) and who, having finished that work, has rejoined him.

What is odd is that Paul says nothing about these two except what he has previously said about Demas: not even the word *gone* is repeated in the original. The words that describe Demas are expected to apply to these two as well. So what Paul actually says is, *Demas has deserted me and gone to Thessalonica, Crescens to Galatia, Titus to Dalmatia,* which reads uncomfortably close to the idea that three men have deserted Paul, not one. Of course, it is only the word *gone* which needs to be supplied, and it is not necessary to infer that Crescens and Titus are deserters too – but it is frighteningly plausible. Especially given that the following section describes someone Paul has *sent*, and Paul could have mentioned Crescens and Titus there.

On the most optimistic reading, Paul still sent out church workers from Rome, and despite the disappointment over Demas that practice would continue. On the most pessimistic reading, that disappointment includes three men, not one, but the task of sending out workers is unchanged. The very fact that we are discussing whether Titus has defected, and that such an idea should be plausible within the context of 2 Timothy, shows how the lessons of this letter are needed. Christian leaders, no matter how mature and long-serving, are always to be nurtured, prayed for and watched. If Demas could falter, so could anyone. Even Timothy.

LUKE

Paul does not mean there was no-one else apart from Luke in Rome with him (4:21), but that there was no one else of his trained workers with him. This is important for a correct reading of this section. Paul is not jotting down the travel arrangements for a few friends, nor even plaintively commenting on his own loneliness, but tracking the complex and interlocking movements of a team. Hence the next step.

MARK

Mark had been a valued member of Paul's group until a disagreement in Cyprus, but had carried on in the church planting work with Barnabas (Acts 13–14). There has obviously been some reconciliation in the past, because Mark is simply to be collected on the way and brought to Rome with Timothy.

The reason is that Paul finds Mark *helpful to me in my ministry*. The word *my* has crept into the translation here which is not in the original and masks what Paul wrote. It makes it sound as if Paul wanted Mark to do some personal errands for him. But without the word *my*, the sentence has a different feel altogether, and sounds again as if Paul is collecting his team together: *Get Mark and bring him with you, because he is helpful to me in ministry* (4:11).

TICHYCUS

Here is another member of the team. He had travelled with Paul on his last journey to Jerusalem (Acts 20:4), and carried the letters to Ephesus (Ephesians 6:21) and Colossae (Colossians 4:7), and possibly to Titus in Crete (Titus 3:12). Now he is on the way to Ephesus, where Timothy is reading this letter. The reason he is travelling in one direction, from Rome to Ephesus, is presumably to free Timothy to travel in the opposite direction.

TIMOTHY

Paul's desire to make Timothy stand firm in his ministry was not with the intention that he should remain rooted in Ephesus, but that with his courage strengthened he was to travel to Rome, bringing Mark, and some clothes and books from Troas.

There are a number ways of reading this series of movements. The first and most usual is to continue with the understanding of Paul on the brink of death, alone, anxious and cold. So he gathers his closest and dearest friends together for one last time, and prepares them for the inevitable.

There is a strong echo of this understanding in a letter sent by the Reformer, John Wycliffe, from his prison in Vilvorde, near Brussels in Belgium, in 1535. 'I entreat your Lordship, and that by the Lord Jesus, that if I must remain here for the winter you would beg the Commissary to be so kind as to send me, from the things of mine which he has, a warmer cap; I feel the cold painfully in my head. Also, a warmer cloak, for the cloak I have is very thin. He has a woollen shirt of mine, if he will send it. But most of all, my Hebrew Bible, Grammar and vocabulary, that I may spend my time in that pursuit.' It is a moving letter, and a challenge to comfortable and lazy ministers today. But its similarity to Paul's request, and the fact that it is so often quoted in commentaries, should make us pause to ask if perhaps the letter from Wycliffe might not have exercised too strong a control on the imagination of those explaining the letter from Paul.

An alternative has been suggested, which is much more robust and plausible, but requires a rethinking of Paul's friends, needs and circumstances. The people he is collecting are not just close friends and loved brothers in Christ, but his experienced and trusted team. If this letter has its effect, Paul will have in Rome Luke, Mark and Timothy, a powerful combination of talented leaders. His needs are simple but important: his cloak would have been of thick wool, far too heavy for wearing or even carrying in a Mediterranean summer but ideally warm and dry for the winter. It was obviously a good one, because he could have asked one of his people in Rome to have bought him a cheap replacement. From the fact that it was left for the summer with other bulky materials in Troas (either because he was arrested there or because Carpus had suitable storage space) its normal use becomes clear: it was a travelling cloak. His library also has to be brought, not only the Scriptures but possibly copies of his church correspondence, records of what he had said and thought, and so on. Timothy has to bring a combination of study and filing cabinet.

At the least, this argues for a dynamic view of Paul in prison. If he is expecting the trial to continue, then he is going to fight it, and those documents Timothy brings might be crucial in his defence against the charge of causing revolution by his teaching. The gathering together of a team means that if he expects to be spending a large part, or even the rest of his life in prison, then he will charge these capable leaders with the task of continuing to spread the gospel. Paul still has the mission to the world on his heart, even if it is the next generation which has to take the next step.

And might it be possible that he expected to win his case? After all, he has come through the first stage intact and vindicated (4:17). Perhaps it would all be over quickly, and Timothy will have to make haste to come before the sea traffic closed for winter (4:21). That travelling cloak might yet come in handy.

A wildly optimistic reading of Paul's plans, in which Paul's expected *departure* (4:6) was his release from prison has been suggested by some, but found to be implausible. The situation in Rome was too difficult for that, and Paul's vocabulary argues for understanding him to mean his death there (see section 27 on 4:6). The fact that Paul knew that his death was not merely inevitable but close, and that he has the task of handing on the baton to the next group of workers, does not necessarily mean that he was going to die within the next few days. Those travel plans would take some time to carry out. The most likely scenario is that whether or not Paul expected to be executed, he certainly expected to die, and he gathered his team, possibly for a farewell, but also to make strategic plans for the years ahead, for reaching the unreached people and training for the future. Paul has already told Timothy to take a long view in the training of his co-workers (2:2); perhaps, here, we see the same lesson being applied by the apostle himself.

STUDY, DISCUSSION AND PRAYER

1. Think of the area where you live – where are the unreached areas and people who need to hear the Christian message? How are you going to do it?

2. Who are the discouraged leaders in your church? How could you bring them together to renew their sense of purpose?

3. Pray for those unreached areas and those discouraged leaders. Pray that you might be empowered by God's Spirit to serve these people.

29

A loyal Lord

4:16–18

Far from being a gentle winding down to the letter, these verses are the final explanation of Paul's thought which he outlined in 4:1. Verse 18 could even claim to be the climax of the whole letter. There are three themes to notice, and they encapsulate many of the thoughts so far.

THE HIGH PRICE OF LOYALTY AS A CHRISTIAN

It is obvious from verse 16 that the Christians in Rome had deserted Paul, in addition to the Asian Christians, and Demas with a few others (4:10), when they refused to come to Paul's support in court (1:15). *Everyone deserted me.* Again, that is superficially untrue because he still knows *Eubulus, Pudens, Linus, Claudia and all the brothers* (4:21), but it is true in the particular sense that Paul needed a character witness, a *patronus,* who would stand by his side and testify that he was upright and innocent. Every one of his potential helpers in Rome had become nervous at the thought of making a public profession of friendship with such a discreditable man. They are still Christians, and Paul's prayer that it *may ... not be held against them* is remarkably generous in the circumstances. It may have been a conscious effort to follow Jesus' own attitude at his execution (Luke 23:34).

So Paul reminds Timothy that opposition and desertion are not passing fads in the church, nor are they indicators that the church is in terminal decline. Rather, they are the constant reality that every church will see as each generation is called to pay a price for its discipleship, and some find the price too high to pay. If Timothy stays loyal to Paul he will find himself on occasion deserted by his Christian friends, and opposed by his Christian ex-friends. And so will we, unless we join the deserters.

THE WONDERFUL PRESENCE OF GOD WITH CHRISTIANS

Although he had been deserted, Paul was not alone. Standing in the court alongside him, where his Christian friends should have been standing, was *the Lord,* the best character witness he could have had. The pattern is repeated again: Paul's suffering means the gospel advances, and his suffering is not a sign that he has been abandoned by God but rather that he is approved. He is given courage to make the most difficult speech of his life, the fulfilment of his ministry to the Gentiles as he testifies in the Emperor's own court, perhaps even before the Emperor himself, to the gospel of grace.

And he survives it. The relief is almost audible as he reports *I was delivered from the lion's mouth.* Possibly, he means that literally, although it would have been highly unusual for a Roman citizen to have been thrown to the lions. Possibly, he could be describing Rome's ferocious power and his escape from it. But he could equally be reflecting a more biblical idea. Psalm 22, the Psalm that Jesus quoted on the cross, asks God to *rescue me from the mouth of the lions* (Psalm 22:21). Or he could be remembering that another man had been on trial before a pagan court for his faith, and he had been thrown to the lions and survived unscathed. As King Darius said of Daniel's God, *he rescues and saves; he performs signs and wonders in the heavens and on the earth. He has rescued Daniel from the power of the lions* (Daniel 6:27).

THE GREAT PROMISE OF GOD TO ALL CHRISTIANS

The word translated as *delivered* in verse 17 is the same word translated as *rescue* in verse 18; only the tense has changed. Paul means us to make a close comparison between what has happened to him recently and what will happen in the future, to him and by extension to all Christians.

What sort of attack on Paul would constitute an *evil* one, and what would *rescue* from it look like? Whichever date one chooses for Paul's death, tradition is unanimous that he was executed in Rome. Does that count as an *evil attack*?

Not quite. It is important to identify Paul's goal, which is that the Lord *will bring me safely to his heavenly kingdom.* An *evil attack* will be something that stops him getting there, and although neither torture nor death can do that, what might is something which tempted him, even at this late stage, to become a coward himself, and to desert. But Paul has come this far, and come through so much, that he can be confident that God will not allow that to happen. Nothing can stop God's plan of getting Christians into heaven. He wrote so that Timothy, having his eyes fixed on that *heavenly kingdom,* and not being deflected by loving *this world* (4:10), will share that confidence.

THE CLIMAX

The theme of the future has run through this letter, literally from its start (1:1) to its finish, here, with God receiving *glory for ever and ever.* So has the continual note of warning, from 1:7–8 to here. If we lose the authentic Christian view of the future, of Jesus' return and eternal reign in glory, all else falls apart.

Will we work for the crowd (4:3) or the crown (4:8)?

Will our lives be marked by patience or pettiness?

Will we be willing to endure hardship (4:5) or would we rather enjoy pleasure (3:4)?

STUDY, DISCUSSION AND PRAYER

1. Can you understand why people might prefer to desert Paul? How can you ensure that you will not?

2. If you are facing a hard time, how do you want other Christians to pray for you?

3. What kind of evil attacks do you fear? How might they stop you entering God's kingdom?

4. What has been the hardest time for you as a Christian? How did you know God stood with you?

5. Pray for someone you know facing a hard time, that they would not be stopped from entering God's kingdom and that they would be strengthened to continue to 'finish the race'.

30

Friends

4:19–22

In this last section Paul is finally exchanging news which has little to do with his main purpose in writing. It comes after the final *Amen* of 4:18, and in a similar way to Philippians 4:21–23, it provides space for some less essential news of people Timothy knew. Priscilla and Aquila, Paul's long-standing co-workers, are to be greeted, perhaps because they are the kind of friends Timothy should be cultivating to keep him firm. Erastus was back in his home town of Corinth. Timothy would have been glad of news of him because he was an old colleague (Acts 19:22) and, like Timothy himself, could have been no use as a witness in Rome because the two of them had left Ephesus before the riot. Trophimus, who was from Ephesus (Acts 21:29) and had worked with Timothy, Paul and Tichycus (Acts 20:4), was sick, unable to travel with Paul to Rome and unable to travel back home to be with Timothy. To encourage Timothy to travel speedily, Paul tells him of the Christians in Rome who are longing to see him. Relationships were important to these early Christians, and their mutual encouragement would have been sorely needed as the difficulties of being a believer increased.

The last two sentences of the letter are important, because they show the potential readership of a letter addressed primarily to those who are responsible for churches. *The Lord be with your spirit,* prays Paul, perhaps wanting God to stand by Timothy as he had stood by him (4:17), and perhaps wanting Timothy to know that he did not pastor alone (2:11–13). *Grace be with you* is addressed in the plural, because Paul expects the church to read the letter as well as Timothy. They need to know the pressures that their leaders face, and their leaders need to know that their churches understand, and will support them and expect them to stay true. Timothy was normal. That, then, is the value of reading 2 Timothy in our churches today.

STUDY, DISCUSSION AND PRAYER

1. How would you summarise the message of 2 Timothy?

2. Can you think of people that you need to encourage with its message?

Living the Bible Today studies

Interactive studies linking knowledge and application

Amos
Hope beyond Judgment
Paul Barker

Haggai and Malachi
Now or Never
Tim Foster

Luke
Towards the Cross
David Hewetson

John 13-17
The Final Farewell
Tracy Lauersen

Ephesians
Know and Live
Stephen Hale

Colossians
New Life, New Lifestyle
Stephen Hale

James
Believe and Behave
David Hewetson

Revelation
The Big Picture
Tim Foster

Reading the Bible Today commentaries

Presenting careful scholarship from respected authors

Proverbs
The Tree of Life
Graeme Goldsworthy

Daniel
Kingdoms in Conflict
Andrew Reid

Mark
The Servant King
Paul Barnett

Romans
Dust to Destiny
David Seccombe

Hebrews
The Majestic Son
Peter Adam

Revelation
Apocalypse Now and Then
Paul Barnett